3·MINUTE
DEVOTIONS
FOR A
Thankful Heart

3·MINUTE
DEVOTIONS
FOR A

Thankful Heart

180 READINGS FOR WOMEN

BARBOUR
PUBLISHING

© 2021 by Barbour Publishing, Inc.

ISBN 978-1-63609-726-8

Text originally appeared in *Choose Gratitude: 3-Minute Devotions for Women*, published by Barbour Publishing, Inc.

Cover Design: Greg Jackson, Thinkpen Design

Published by Barbour Publishing, Inc., 1810 Barbour Drive, Uhrichsville, Ohio 44683, www.barbourbooks.com

Our mission is to inspire the world with the life-changing message of the Bible.

Member of the
Evangelical Christian
Publishers Association

Printed in China.

Choose Gratitude Today!

Thankfulness is woven through the pages of the Bible. The medical and psychological professions also agree that gratitude has spiritual significance. According to a Harvard Medical School newsletter, "With gratitude, people acknowledge the goodness in their lives. . . . As a result, being grateful also helps people connect to something larger than themselves as individuals—whether to other people, nature, or a higher power."[*] Alex Wood, a psychologist at Sterling University, writes that gratitude is "also a habitual focusing on and appreciating the positive aspects of life."[†] And psychologist Robert Emmons, one of the leading scientific experts on gratitude, has gone so far as to say that gratitude is even a form of love.[‡] So take it from the experts—a thankful heart is good for the soul! It will bring you closer to God and to others, and it will lead you into a more joyful way of living.

[*] "Giving Thanks Can Make You Happier," *HEALTHbeat*, August 14, 2021, www.health.harvard.edu/healthbeat/giving-thanks-can-make-you-happier.

[†] Alex M. Wood, Jeffrey J. Froh, and Adam W. A. Geraghty, "Gratitude and Well-Being: A Review and Theoretical Integration," *Clinical Psychology Review* 30, no. 7 (November 2010): 890–905.

[‡] Robert Emmons, "Why Gratitude Is Good," *Greater Good*, November 16, 2010, https://greatergood.berkeley.edu/article/item/why_gratitude_is_good.

I will give You thanks with all my heart;
I will sing praises to You before the gods.
I will bow down toward Your holy temple
and give thanks to Your name for Your
lovingkindness and Your truth; for You have
magnified Your word according to all Your
name. On the day I called, You answered me;
You made me bold with strength in my soul.

PSALM 138:1–3 NASB

Always

We accept it always, and in all places. . .with all thankfulness.

ACTS 24:3 KJV

Sometimes we think of gratitude as a polite sort of feeling. After all, as children we no doubt were taught to say thank you. But the Bible says that thankfulness is more than being polite. Rather, it is an essential aspect of our lives. We need to learn to consciously cultivate it so that it becomes the framework of our daily lives. Each thing—each person, each event, each place, even each animal—that enters our lives is a gift from a God who loves us so deeply and intimately that we will never be able to grasp the extent of His love, at least not in this life. And so we greet each aspect of our lives not only with acceptance but with thankfulness.

LORD OF LOVE, THANK YOU FOR YOUR MANY GIFTS. HELP ME TO SEE YOUR LOVE EVEN IN THE THINGS THAT SEEM HARD. HELP ME TO CULTIVATE A CONSTANT ATTITUDE OF GRATITUDE.

Richness

Let the message about Christ, in all its richness,
fill your lives. . . . Sing psalms and hymns and
spiritual songs to God with thankful hearts.

COLOSSIANS 3:16 NLT

- -

The more we think about Christ and all He has done for us, the more gratitude will fill our lives. Because of His love for us, we not only have eternal life but have a life filled to the brim with blessings right now. Because of Christ, we are free from the guilt and anxiety of sin. Because of Christ, we can come close to God; we even have God living within our hearts, knit into the fabric of our being. The more we ponder this reality, the more the richness of our lives in Christ just naturally spills over into a song of thankfulness.

I AM SO GRATEFUL, CHRIST, FOR THE IMMENSE RICHNESS OF ALL YOU HAVE DONE FOR ME. MAY MY LIFE BE FILLED WITH SONGS OF PRAISE TO YOU.

Roots

Let your roots grow down into him, and let your lives be built on him. Then your faith will grow strong in the truth you were taught, and you will overflow with thankfulness.

COLOSSIANS 2:7 NLT

Life is uncertain. Our world is full of so many dangers, so much unrest, so many arguments, and so much fear and anger. In the midst of all that, it can be hard to keep our balance. It's easy to feel as though we're at sea in the middle of a storm, being tossed back and forth. But the Bible tells us we don't have to live like that. Instead, we can grow deep roots anchored firmly in God. When our lives are built on Him, we will no longer lose our balance because of the world's dangers and unrest. Our faith will grow strong—and our hearts will overflow with thankfulness.

GOD, I AM SO GRATEFUL THAT YOU ARE HELPING ME TO GROW DEEP ROOTS IN YOU. I KNOW THAT NO MATTER WHAT IS HAPPENING IN THE WORLD, I DON'T NEED TO BE AFRAID.

Food

*God created those foods to be eaten with thanks
by faithful people who know the truth.*
1 Timothy 4:3 nlt

- -

We live in a world where both dieting and overeating are like the two sides of a double-edged sword. Our society tells us we need to be thin; we need to look a certain way in order to measure up (and most of us have bumps and bulges that we wish would go away). At the same time, food—and a lot of it—plays a very important role in our social activities. Often we turn to food when we are bored or sad or nervous, and then we feel guilty and anxious because we believe we should be eating less. The Bible, however, points us in a different direction when it comes to food. Food is a gift from God, and we are to give thanks for it. It's that simple.

LORD, HEAL MY ATTITUDES TOWARD FOOD.
MAY I REMEMBER THAT EACH THING I EAT
IS A GIFT FROM YOU. TAKE AWAY BOTH
MY OVERINDULGENCE AND MY GUILT, AND
REPLACE THEM WITH THANKFULNESS.

Good

For everything created by God is good, and nothing
is to be rejected if it is received with gratitude.

1 TIMOTHY 4:4 NASB

When God created the world, He declared that each thing He made was good. Too often, however, we human beings have abused or misused the good things God created. We overindulge in ways that harm both our bodies and creation. Or we swing the other way and erect rules and boundaries around certain things, denying ourselves for no good reason. The Bible gives us a middle road between these two extremes. When gratitude becomes the light in which we live, we will find ourselves able to live in moderation, accepting God's goodness without selfishness or greed.

LOVING LORD, THANK YOU FOR YOUR WONDERFUL CREATION. TEACH ME TO HONOR IT. MAY EACH THING I DO, WHETHER IT'S EATING, DRIVING MY CAR, OR BUYING CLOTHES, BE TO YOUR GLORY.

Unshakable

Therefore, since we receive a kingdom which cannot be shaken, let us show gratitude, by which we may offer to God an acceptable service with reverence and awe.

HEBREWS 12:28 NASB

- -

Our emotions go up and down. Even within a single day, we may shift from joy to sorrow, from laughter to anger. Emotions are a normal and healthy part of being human, but we don't need to let them rule our lives. Gratitude can be the steady thread that keeps us tied firmly to the kingdom of God, a reality that never changes. In the midst of each feeling we experience, a sense of thankfulness will keep us from shaking. At times we may struggle to feel thankful, but as we consciously practice our awareness of God's presence, gratitude will become a habit that holds us steady through all our emotions.

OH GOD OF POWER AND MIGHT, MAY I NEVER LOSE SIGHT OF YOUR AMAZING REALITY. MAY MY GRATITUDE TO YOU BE THE UNDERLYING BEDROCK OF ALL I FEEL.

Trust

The LORD is my strength and shield. I trust him with all my heart. He helps me, and my heart is filled with joy. I burst out in songs of thanksgiving.
PSALM 28:7 NLT

- -

Gratitude and trust are intimately linked together. The more we trust God, the more thankful we will feel for His love and care. The more we practice thankfulness for all God has done and is doing in our lives, the more we will trust Him. The two things just naturally go together. God helps us with our daily lives—and our hearts spontaneously spill over with joy and gratitude. Living in this state of continual glad thankfulness takes practice, though. We can choose to dwell on all that is "wrong" with our lives—or we can choose to see life from the perspective of trust and gratitude.

TEACH ME, I PRAY, TO TRUST YOU MORE, LORD.
HELP ME TO SEE ALL THAT YOU ARE
DOING IN MY LIFE. MAY MY HEART BURST
OUT IN SONGS OF GRATITUDE.

Worry

Don't worry about anything; instead, pray about everything.
Tell God what you need, and thank him for all he has done.
PHILIPPIANS 4:6 NLT

Did you know that the very earliest Old English meaning of *worry* was "to strangle"? It literally meant "to seize by the throat and tear." That's how destructive worry can be. It can rip away our sense of peace and well-being. It can make us lose sleep and rob our days of joy. But the Bible says there is an antidote to worry: prayer and gratitude. The more we pray about our concerns, giving them to God and thanking Him for His work in our lives, the less room we will have in our minds for worry. Anxiety and gratitude can't exist in the same place in our heads.

HEAVENLY FATHER, WHEN WORRY BEGINS
TO CONSUME MY MIND, REMIND ME THAT
THERE'S A WAY OUT. TURN MY ATTENTION
TO PRAYER AND GRATITUDE.

Joyful Noise

Let us come before his presence with thanksgiving,
and make a joyful noise unto him with psalms.
PSALM 95:2 KJV

Thankfulness is an inner feeling—but to have its full effect in us, it needs to spill over into our outer lives where others can see it. There are all kinds of ways we can make a "joyful noise." It might be a song we hum while we do our work, but it could just as easily be a note of happiness that others can hear in our voices when we speak. Many times it won't be a literal noise. It might be the ease with which we laugh, or even just a smile on our faces. It could be words we write in emails or texts or the lightness of our feet as we go about our work.

I WANT TO LIVE MY LIFE IN YOUR PRESENCE, DEAR GOD, A PLACE THAT PUTS A SONG ON MY LIPS, A SMILE ON MY FACE, AND A DANCE IN MY STEP.

Communal Thanksgiving

All this is for your benefit, so that the grace that is reaching more and more people may cause thanksgiving to overflow to the glory of God.

2 CORINTHIANS 4:15 NIV

God is good to each of us individually, and we each have our own unique relationship with Him. This means that gratitude may be a private, individual feeling we carry in our hearts. At the same time, though, we are called to live in community, and the Holy Spirit spreads grace to us all. In this sense, gratitude is communal. It's something we experience together, and it's something we express together. As we do, we amplify gratitude. We feel it more intensely as individuals—and it spreads from us to others.

THANK YOU, LORD OF LOVE, THAT YOUR GRACE HAS NO LIMITS. MAY IT SPILL THROUGH ME TO OTHERS. MAKE US, I PRAY, A COMMUNITY KNIT TOGETHER BY GRATITUDE.

The Gateway to God's Presence

Enter into his gates with thanksgiving, and into his courts with praise: be thankful unto him, and bless his name.

PSALM 100:4 KJV

Sometimes we get the idea that God's presence is a solemn, sober place, a place with few smiles and little laughter. When we give others that impression, following Christ doesn't look like much fun. The Bible tells us, though, that the gate into God's presence is the practice of joyful thanksgiving. Gratitude is the certain entryway into His courts. The more we thank Him, the closer we will draw to Him. The more we praise Him, the more we will be aware of His sure and constant presence in our lives.

THANK YOU, GOD, FOR ALL YOU DO FOR ME. THANK YOU FOR YOUR LOVE. THANK YOU FOR YOUR CONTINUAL PRESENCE. TEACH ME TO ALWAYS BLESS YOUR NAME.

Multiplied

"There will be joy and songs of thanksgiving, and I will multiply my people, not diminish them; I will honor them, not despise them. . . . You will be my people, and I will be your God."

JEREMIAH 30:19, 22 NLT

Sometimes we talk about following Christ as though it were all about giving up things. We act as though the Christian life consists of "don'ts" and "shall nots." But the Bible assures us that God doesn't want to diminish our lives. Instead, He wants to expand them. He wants to multiply our blessings. When we fully realize that we are God's and He is ours, then we will begin to see His love everywhere we turn. And the more we express our gratitude to Him, the sharper our spiritual vision will become.

LORD, I WANT TO SING YOU A SONG OF THANKSGIVING FOR ALL THE WAYS YOU HAVE BLESSED AND MULTIPLIED MY LIFE.

Thankful Talk

*Though some tongues just love the taste of gossip,
those who follow Jesus have better uses for language
than that. Don't talk dirty or silly. That kind of talk
doesn't fit our style. Thanksgiving is our dialect.*

EPHESIANS 5:3–4 MSG

- -

An attitude of thanksgiving pushes out a lot of temptations, including the temptation to gossip and backbite. It's all too easy to complain about someone behind their back or to share a juicy bit of gossip. But the Bible speaks sternly about careless and unloving talk like this—and it shows us another way. When our conversation is full of words of gratitude, we won't have time for gossip and empty small talk. It may take time and practice, but eventually we'll learn the dialect of thanksgiving and we'll no longer indulge in careless, hurtful conversations.

WHENEVER I BEGIN TO GOSSIP, COMPLAIN,
OR ENGAGE IN THOUGHTLESS, SILLY WORDS,
REMIND ME, LORD, THAT YOU ARE CALLING
ME TO LEARN A NEW LANGUAGE.

An Enduring Foundation

With praise and thanksgiving they sang to the L*ORD*: *"He is good; his love toward Israel endures forever." And all the people gave a great shout of praise to the* L*ORD*, *because the foundation of the house of the* L*ORD* *was laid.*

E*ZRA* 3:11 *NIV*

What do you consider the foundation of your life to be? We all rely on different things—family, friends, money, careers, our homes— and while these things aren't bad in themselves, none of them will endure. Family and friends will die, money comes and goes, careers come to an end, homes are temporary shelters. Only God is a firm foundation that endures forever. When we rely on Him as the foundation that underlies all the other aspects of our lives, then we can go through life with a sense of joyful gratitude. Our home will be His unchanging presence.

> MY HEART AND SOUL SHOUT FOR JOY TO YOU, OH LORD, THE FOUNDATION OF MY LIFE, FOR YOUR LOVE ENDURES FOREVER.

All People!

I urge, then, first of all, that petitions, prayers, intercession and thanksgiving be made for all people.

1 TIMOTHY 2:1 NIV

- -

Most of us can think of at least one individual in our life who is difficult to like. The Bible never says we have to like everybody— but it does say we need to pray for everyone, even those people who are so hard to put up with. It's one thing, though, to pray for these individuals, asking God to help them and bless them. But the Bible goes one step further and says we are also to be *thankful* for these people. That may seem like a real challenge when it comes to some people. How can we be thankful for people who get on our nerves? And what about people who are cruel or lack integrity? The Bible doesn't give us any wiggle room here, though. As we form a habit of praying and thanking God for *all people*, we may find we begin to see them differently.

LORD, I ASK THAT YOU BE WITH THE INDIVIDUALS
I FIND DIFFICULT TO LIKE. BLESS THEM. HEAL
THEM. STRENGTHEN THEM IN YOUR LOVE.
THANK YOU FOR MAKING THESE PEOPLE.
HELP ME TO SEE THEM WITH YOUR EYES.

Completion

When it came time for the dedication of the wall, they tracked down and brought in the Levites from all their homes in Jerusalem to carry out the dedication with exuberance: thanksgiving hymns, songs, cymbals, harps, and lutes.

NEHEMIAH 12:27 MSG

During the time that God's people lived in exile, the city of Jerusalem had fallen into ruins. When Nehemiah heard the news, he felt called by God to go back to Jerusalem and rebuild the wall around the city. It was a huge task that involved overcoming political opposition as well as putting in days of careful planning followed by hard, sweaty labor. When the wall was completed, Nehemiah must have felt a huge sense of satisfaction—but instead of allowing his pride to turn into an ego trip, he immediately dedicated his work to God. He turned the completion of this immense project into an opportunity for an exuberant celebration of thanksgiving.

REMIND ME, LORD, TO DEDICATE EACH PROJECT I UNDERTAKE TO YOU. MAY EACH TASK I COMPLETE BE A REMINDER OF YOUR GENEROUS GRACE.

All Circumstances

Give thanks in all circumstances; for this is
God's will for you in Christ Jesus.

1 THESSALONIANS 5:18 NIV

- -

We are used to thinking of thankfulness as something we feel only in circumstances we label as "good." We thank God for a loved one's healing, for a salary raise, or for the birth of a child. We are less likely to feel gratitude at the death of a loved one, the loss of a job, or a chronic illness that just won't go away. But the Bible tells us to give thanks in *all* circumstances. This doesn't mean we're expected to feel happy about hard or tragic events. God doesn't ask us to deny our sorrow, anger, or disappointment. But even in the midst of those feelings, we can choose to say thank You to God, knowing that even now He is working in our lives.

HELP ME, JESUS, TO SAY THANK
YOU EVEN WHEN IT'S HARD.

The Holy Spirit

Be filled with the Holy Spirit, singing psalms and hymns and spiritual songs among yourselves, and making music to the Lord in your hearts. And give thanks for everything to God the Father in the name of our Lord Jesus Christ.

EPHESIANS 5:18–20 NLT

When we choose to practice gratitude, we invite the Holy Spirit into our lives. As we sing out our thanks, both together in community and alone as individuals, we are making room in our hearts for the Spirit to fill us. The Spirit in turn brings a sense of peace and joy that underlies even the hard things in our lives. Filled with the Holy Spirit, we find that gratitude becomes easier to practice. But it all begins with our choice—to practice thanksgiving instead of worry, to praise instead of complain, and to sing instead of curse.

TEACH ME, FAITHFUL FRIEND, TO GIVE
THANKS ALWAYS AND FOR EVERYTHING.

Alertness

*Devote yourselves to prayer, keeping alert in
it with an attitude of thanksgiving.*

COLOSSIANS 4:2 NASB

Jesus promised us that His yoke is easy, not heavy to carry (Matthew 11:30), and the life of a Christian is not meant to be hard. That doesn't mean, though, that we can get careless and sloppy about our calling to be people of God. If we do, we will all too easily slip back into worry, resentment, gossiping, complaining, overindulgence, and all sorts of other unhealthy and unloving practices. The Bible reminds us to stay alert—to pay attention and be careful that we are staying close to God in our hearts and lives. How do we do that? By praying daily and constantly maintaining an attitude of thanksgiving.

I WANT TO STAY ALERT, LORD, SO REMIND
ME THAT I CAN'T AFFORD TO STOP
PRAYING OR PRACTICING GRATITUDE.

Thanksgiving Sacrifices

You called out to GOD in your desperate condition; he got you out in the nick of time. He spoke the word that healed you, that pulled you back from the brink of death. So thank GOD for his marvelous love, for his miracle mercy to the children he loves; offer thanksgiving sacrifices, tell the world what he's done—sing it out!

PSALM 107:18–22 MSG

We have come to think that to sacrifice means "to give up something." The original meaning of sacrifice, however, was "to offer something to God." The Bible tells us that the sacrifice God wants most from us is that of thanksgiving. Not because it's something hard or painful to do, but because by offering our gratitude to God, we enrich our lives. We learn to see God's mercy at work in our world. We expand our sense of joy. We come to realize the reality of His marvelous love. So sing it out! Don't keep it to yourself. Tell the world all the amazing things God has done.

GOD OF POWER AND GRACE, I WANT TO OFFER YOU A SACRIFICE OF THANKSGIVING. MAY I NOT SAVE THIS SACRIFICE FOR SPECIAL OCCASIONS, BUT INSTEAD MAY IT BE MY DAILY PRACTICE.

Faithful Love

Hallelujah! Give thanks to the Lord, for He is good; His faithful love endures forever.

PSALM 106:1 HCSB

- - - - - - - - - - - - - - - - - -

Even the most devoted spouse or oldest friend can let us down. They may not mean to or want to, but humans make mistakes; they're not perfect, and it would be unrealistic to expect them to be. That doesn't keep our feelings from being hurt, though! And it hurts even worse when someone we love intentionally turns their back on us. But God will never do that. Unlike human beings, He has no limits to His love. His faithfulness endures forever. And that's good reason to thank Him!

THANK YOU, DEAREST LORD, FOR YOUR LOVE
THAT NEVER FAILS. THANK YOU THAT NO
MATTER WHAT HAPPENS, I CAN RELY ON YOU.

Hand in Hand

Let the peace that comes from Christ rule in your hearts. For as members of one body you are called to live in peace. And always be thankful.

COLOSSIANS 3:15 NLT

Paul, the author of this scripture passage, is letting us in on a secret here. The peace that comes from Christ, the peace that passes all human understanding, is connected to thankfulness. The more we thank God for everything, both the lovely things and the hard things, the lovable people and the not-so-lovable ones, the more we will experience the peace of Christ. Gratitude is an effective tool for sweeping the anxiety out of our hearts. Complaining and feeling dissatisfied—behaviors that are the opposite of thankfulness—lead to anxiety, stress, and resentment. But peace and gratitude go hand in hand.

LORD, HELP ME TO FORM A HABIT OF
THANKFULNESS. I WANT TO LIVE IN YOUR PEACE.

Jesus' Representative

And whatever you do or say, do it as a representative of the Lord Jesus, giving thanks through him to God the Father.

COLOSSIANS 3:17 NLT

Making a conscious effort to act and speak the way Jesus would radically changes the way we live our lives. It's not easy. It takes practice and attention. But one way to make it easier is to build the habit of thanking Jesus for being with us moment by moment. Sometimes we may not be able to sense His presence—but thanking Him anyway, regardless of our perceptions, builds our confidence. It helps us to stay on track. We have a greater sense of His companionship with us through all of our lives' challenges and joys. He walks with us and guides our choices so that we can be good representatives of His love.

I WANT TO BE YOUR REPRESENTATIVE, LORD JESUS.
THANK YOU THAT YOU ARE ALWAYS WITH ME.

Magnifying Glasses

I will praise the name of God with a song,
and will magnify him with thanksgiving.

PSALM 69:30 KJV

When we praise God and offer Him our thanks, we become like transparent glass. All our selfishness and self-centered concerns get out of the way. As the light of God shines through us, we magnify that light. We enable others to see it more easily. We even enable ourselves to see it more easily. The more we praise and thank God, the more clearly we will see His light shining into the darkness of our lives. So go ahead—sing a song of thanksgiving to the Lord. Whether you can carry a tune really doesn't matter!

THANK YOU, GOD, FOR ALL YOU HAVE DONE
FOR ME. I WANT TO MAGNIFY YOUR LIGHT.

Keeping Our Promises

What can I give back to God for the blessings he's poured
out on me? I'll lift high the cup of salvation—a toast to God!
I'll pray in the name of God; I'll complete what I promised
God I'd do, and I'll do it together with his people.... Oh, God,
here I am, your servant, your faithful servant: set me free for
your service! I'm ready to offer the thanksgiving sacrifice and
pray in the name of God. I'll complete what I promised God
I'd do, and I'll do it in company with his people, in the place of
worship, in God's house, in Jerusalem, God's city. Hallelujah!

PSALM 116:12–19 MSG

One way we can express our gratitude to God is by keeping our promises to Him. But God doesn't expect us to do this alone. Not only do we have the support of God's people, but we also have His Spirit within us, setting us free for God's service. With that help from within and without, we can follow through on our promises to God, offering Him a sacrifice of thanksgiving and love.

SET ME FREE, LORD, SO THAT I CAN
SERVE YOU. I AM SO GRATEFUL FOR
ALL YOU HAVE DONE FOR ME.

Intercession

We give thanks to God always for you all,
making mention of you in our prayers.

1 THESSALONIANS 1:2 KJV

- -

There are several different kinds of prayers, from praise to petitions to intercession. Intercession is when we pray on behalf of another person. The Bible makes clear that this type of prayer is a normal and necessary part of following Jesus. We regularly, perhaps even daily, pray for the people in our lives, asking God to bless and help them. There's an aspect of intercession that we don't always consider, though—thanksgiving. Not only do we ask God's blessing on others, but we also thank Him for these individuals. We may be surprised to find that as a result our relationships with others change and deepen.

HEAVENLY FRIEND, I THANK YOU FOR EACH
OF THE PEOPLE YOU HAVE PUT IN MY LIFE.

Victory over Death

"Death has been swallowed up in victory." "Where, O death, is your victory? Where, O death, is your sting?" The sting of death is sin, and the power of sin is the law. But thanks be to God! He gives us the victory through our Lord Jesus Christ.

1 CORINTHIANS 15:54–57 NIV

God has given us so many reasons to feel grateful. The fact that we no longer have to be afraid of death is just one more reason, but it's a pretty big reason! Through Jesus, death no longer has the last word. The thing that most people fear more than anything no longer has to strike terror into our hearts. In Christ, we will live forever. He has conquered death, and so humanity's age-old enemy no longer has any power over us. Thanks be to God!

LORD JESUS, THANK YOU THAT ON THE CROSS YOU GAVE US VICTORY OVER DEATH. I AM SO GRATEFUL THAT I NO LONGER NEED TO BE AFRAID OF DYING. DEATH WILL NOT BE AN ENDING BUT INSTEAD A DOORWAY INTO ETERNITY.

Indescribable

Thanks be to God for his indescribable gift!
2 CORINTHIANS 9:15 NIV

- -

Words are important. How we use them shapes the way we see reality. The more we speak words of gratitude rather than complaints, the more joy we will feel. But sometimes words fail us. God has given us so much, and we can try to describe His many gifts with words—but when it comes right down to it, God's love and blessing are too big for any words to fully express. The Creator of the universe called each one of us into being, and He sustains each of our lives with His love. How can we even wrap our brains around that, let alone put it into words? All we can do is say thank You.

THANK YOU, GOD. I DON'T KNOW WHAT ELSE TO SAY, SO I'LL JUST SAY IT AGAIN: THANK YOU!

Good Gifts

Every good and perfect gift is from above,
coming down from the Father of the heavenly lights,
who does not change like shifting shadows.

JAMES 1:17 NIV

In this verse, James reminds us that each good thing in our lives is actually a gift from God. Sometimes we thank God for "spiritual" things, forgetting that we can find God as well in all the lovely details of life—a child's smile, a good meal, a glimpse of a hummingbird, a beautiful sunset, a starry expanse of nighttime sky, a friend's kindness, a pet's loyalty, the light shining through a tree's leaves—all these are reasons to give thanks to God, for they are all gifts of love given to us from His generous hand. We can give Him thanks for more mundane things as well—a good night's sleep, a debt paid off, a smoothly functioning washing machine. Nothing is too little for our gratitude!

THANK YOU, FATHER, FOR YOUR MANY GIFTS. THANK YOU THAT YOUR GENEROSITY NEVER CHANGES.

Nature

*Sing to GOD a thanksgiving hymn, play music on your
instruments to God, who fills the sky with clouds,
preparing rain for the earth, then turning the mountains
green with grass, feeding both cattle and crows.*

PSALM 147:7–9 MSG

Sometimes we take the world of nature for granted. As the seasons
cycle around, it's all just the background for our busy lives. But
the Bible reminds us to pause and truly *see* God's hand at work in
nature. From the rain that turns the earth green, to the majestic
mountains, to the earth's beasts, to the ever-changing beauty of the
clouds in the sky, our world is filled with loveliness. God has created
a world of vast beauty. When we remember to look around us and
truly appreciate the world of nature, our hearts will spill over with
gratitude to the one who created it all.

THANK YOU, CREATOR GOD, FOR THE
BEAUTIFUL WORLD YOU HAVE GIVEN US.
HELP US TO CARE FOR IT RESPONSIBLY.

Generosity

Yes, you will be enriched in every way so that you can always be generous. And when we take your gifts to those who need them, they will thank God.

2 CORINTHIANS 9:11 NLT

We have a special role to play in spreading a spirit of gratitude. As God gives to us, we have gifts and resources to give to others. The people we give to are in turn grateful. God's generosity creates our gratitude, and then our generosity allows others to be grateful too. It's like a stone dropped in water, its circles rippling out endlessly, creating continuous cycles of generosity and gratitude. This is the normal, healthy life of giving and gratitude to which we are all called by God. God enriches us; we give to others; we are all united in gratitude.

GENEROUS GOD, THANK YOU THAT YOU GIVE TO ME SO THAT I CAN GIVE TO OTHERS.

God's Gates

Shout triumphantly to the LORD, all the earth. Serve the LORD with gladness; come before Him with joyful songs. Acknowledge that Yahweh is God. He made us, and we are His—His people, the sheep of His pasture. Enter His gates with thanksgiving and His courts with praise. Give thanks to Him and praise His name. For Yahweh is good, and His love is eternal; His faithfulness endures through all generations.

PSALM 100:1–5 HCSB

The Bible tells us this is "a psalm of thanksgiving." It outlines how we enter into the gates that lead into God's presence—through praise, through service, through song, through gratitude. These are the entry points into God's "courts," the times and places where we feel His presence most deeply. He has given us so many reasons to feel thankful!

DEAR LORD, HELP ME TO SERVE YOU WITH GLADNESS; TEACH ME TO SING OUT YOUR NAME WITH SONGS OF JOY; LET ME OVERFLOW WITH THANKSGIVING FOR ALL YOU HAVE DONE FOR ME. THANK YOU THAT I AM AMONG THE SHEEP YOU CARE FOR SO TENDERLY. THANK YOU FOR YOUR FAITHFULNESS.

Justice

I will thank the L{\small ORD} because he is just; I will sing
praise to the name of the L{\small ORD} Most High.
P{\small SALM} 7:17 {\small NLT}

Our world often seems lacking in justice. The poor and the marginalized always seem to be with us. Our governments seem less concerned with the needs of ordinary people than with politics and power; and meanwhile, people become more and more polarized, unable to agree on even the simplest things. In the midst of so much confusion, it's good to know that we serve a just God—and ultimately, His justice will prevail. We can praise His name with thanksgiving and gratitude, for His justice, love, and mercy never fail.

JUST GOD, THANK YOU THAT WHEN THE
WORLD SEEMS FULL OF CONFUSION,
YOU ARE STILL IN CONTROL.

Special People

I thank my God every time I remember you.

PHILIPPIANS 1:3 NIV

- -

God has put certain people in our lives who are particular blessings to us. Whether they are friends or family, they are the individuals who have made a difference in who we are. Their love and support have shaped us and helped us to see both God and ourselves more clearly. When we think of these people, our hearts leap with thanksgiving, for these individuals are very special gifts to us from God. He has used them as vehicles for His love. Because of them, we are blessed. With each cherished memory that crosses our minds, we are touched by love and thanksgiving.

GOD, THANK YOU FOR THE SPECIAL PEOPLE IN MY LIFE. MAY MY HEART LEAP UP IN GRATITUDE TO YOU EACH TIME THEY CROSS MY MIND.

Confused

They knew God, but they wouldn't worship him as
God or even give him thanks. And they began to
think up foolish ideas of what God was like. As a
result, their minds became dark and confused.

ROMANS 1:21 NLT

Again and again, the Bible makes clear to us how important gratitude is to our spiritual and emotional well-being. It's not enough to go to church; it's not enough to talk about God or memorize the Bible. We need to have an intimate relationship with Him, one that is based on love and thanksgiving. Without that, everything else is empty—and we are bound to get confused, our thoughts dark and bewildered. But as we worship God, as we lift up our hearts in gratitude for all He has done for us, slowly the light streams back into our lives again. Things become clear once more.

DEAR LORD, I WANT MY RELATIONSHIP WITH YOU
TO BE REAL AND CLOSE. I THANK YOU SO MUCH
FOR EVERYTHING YOU HAVE DONE FOR ME.

Rebuilding

*"I'll turn things around for Jacob. I'll compassionately
come in and rebuild homes. The town will be rebuilt on
its old foundations; the mansions will be splendid again.
Thanksgivings will pour out of the windows; laughter will
spill through the doors. Things will get better and better.
Depression days are over. They'll thrive, they'll flourish."*

JEREMIAH 30:18–19 MSG

The Bible never promises that God's people will experience unending success, wealth, and contentment. Instead, it makes clear that all of us will have times when everything seems to be falling apart. The "buildings" (whether they be actual homes or rather relationships, family roles, or careers) that we constructed so carefully and lovingly seem to fall down around our heads. But God never leaves us there in that state of ruin. The old foundations will be used to build something new. We will laugh with joy once again. We will have reason to be thankful for all that God has done to rebuild our lives.

GOD OF LOVE, WHEN EVERYTHING
SEEMS TO BE FALLING DOWN, REMIND
ME THAT YOU ALWAYS REBUILD.

A Network of Love and Grace

*For all things are for your sakes, so that the grace which
is spreading to more and more people may cause the
giving of thanks to abound to the glory of God.*

2 CORINTHIANS 4:15 NASB

All things are for our sake? That seems like it must be an exaggeration, doesn't it? How can everything that happens be for us? And yet this is what Paul, the author of the letter to the Corinthians, is saying here. In another place, he wrote that all things work together for good (Romans 8:28), and perhaps this is what he means here as well. What's good for me will also be good for you, and what's good for you isn't going to be bad for someone else. Somehow God knits everything together—even the difficult things, even the terrible things—into a network of love and grace that grows and spreads until more and more people are caught up into it.

LORD, MAKE ME AN ACTIVE PARTICIPANT IN
YOUR NETWORK OF LOVE; AND I WILL SPREAD
THANKSGIVING TO EVERYONE I MEET.

Thankful Surrender

Make thankfulness your sacrifice to God.
PSALM 50:14 NLT

- -

When we think about God asking us to make a sacrifice, we imagine that He wants us to give up something we enjoy. We are like Abraham, who believed God wanted him to kill his son on an altar, when what God really wanted wasn't for Abraham to take his son's life but instead to offer him totally to God with joy and thanksgiving. There may be times when God *will* ask us to give up a particular behavior or habit, but only because He knows it's not good for us, not because He likes to take things away from us. Instead, He asks us to dedicate every part of our lives to Him, to stop claiming them for ourselves, and to make thankfulness our daily sacrifice.

THANK YOU, GOD, FOR ALL YOU HAVE GIVEN ME. MAY MY DAILY THANKSGIVING BE AN ACT OF SURRENDER TO YOUR LOVE.

Giving Back

*"Now therefore, our God, we thank You,
and praise Your glorious name."*
1 CHRONICLES 29:13 NASB

The Hebrew word used for "thank" here in the original scripture is an interesting one. It came from a gesture that meant "to throw" or "to cast off." In other words, when we thank God for something, we don't hug it tight to our chest. In fact, we don't even claim it as our own. We give it back to the one who gave it to us. We don't insist on our right to control this gift, but instead we share it with God. Again and again in the Bible, praise and thanksgiving go hand in hand. We can't praise God without feeling gratitude for all He has done. And we can't do either without giving back to God all He has given to us.

LORD, YOU HAVE GIVEN ME SO MUCH.
HELP ME TO GIVE IT ALL BACK TO YOU.

Our Soul

To the end that my glory may sing praise to thee, and not be silent. O LORD my God, I will give thanks unto thee for ever.

PSALM 30:12 KJV

The word that the King James Version of the Bible translates as "glory" also means "soul." It is the part of each of us that makes us who we are; it is the unique light that God placed within us, the thing that makes us shine in our individual ways. This innermost part of our being—our soul—is the place where God calls us to sing out His praises. It is here where gratitude lives within us, making our inner glory gleam with grace as we offer back to God all that He has so generously given to us.

GOD OF GRACE, MAY I SHINE WITH YOUR LOVE AS I GIVE YOU THANKS FOR ALL YOU DO FOR ME.

Focus on the Positive

I will give thanks to you, LORD, with all my heart;
I will tell of all your wonderful deeds.
PSALM 9:1 NIV

One way to build gratitude in our lives and in the lives of others is to focus our speech on the good things God has done for us. Too often when we're talking with our friends, we tend to complain rather than give thanks. We describe the negative things in our lives in great detail while overlooking the positive things, both big and small. The more we feel gratitude in our hearts, the more it will spill out into our conversation. And the reverse is true as well: the more we speak of our gratitude for all life's gifts, the more we will experience thanksgiving in our hearts.

MAY MY SPEECH BE FULL OF THANKSGIVING,
LORD, RATHER THAN COMPLAINTS.

From the Belly of the Whale

"In trouble, deep trouble, I prayed to God. He answered me. From the belly of the grave I cried, 'Help!' You heard my cry. You threw me into ocean's depths, into a watery grave. . . . Yet you pulled me up from that grave alive, O God, my God! . . . I'm worshiping you, God, calling out in thanksgiving! And I'll do what I promised I'd do!"

JONAH 2:1–3, 6, 9 MSG

None of us are likely to be swallowed by a fish the way Jonah was. But we all have times when we feel as though we're trapped somewhere deep in a sea of trouble, and we don't see any way out. Jonah could have been angry with God for putting him through such a terrible ordeal, but instead his thoughts turned to worship and thanksgiving. As it always is, thanksgiving was also an act of surrender for Jonah. It meant that he would no longer rebel against God's plan for his life. Now he would go wherever God told him to go. God had not left him in that smelly, dark place—and now Jonah was ready to serve Him.

LORD, WHEN I FEEL AS THOUGH I'VE BEEN BURIED ALIVE, REMIND ME, EVEN THEN, TO TURN TO YOU IN THANKSGIVING, WITH A NEW WILLINGNESS TO SERVE YOU.

Carriers of God's Grace

I always thank my God for you because of
his grace given you in Christ Jesus.
1 CORINTHIANS 1:4 NIV

Think of the people in your life who bring you joy. Their smiles, their hugs, their understanding, and their unconditional love help to make life worth living. Now consider: Each one of those individuals is a gift from God. Each one carries His grace to you in a unique way. Each one bears Christ Jesus into your life. It's easy to take others for granted—but when we think about the individuals around us in this light, our hearts will overflow with thanksgiving. God brings these special people into our lives to show us how much He loves us.

THANK YOU, JESUS, FOR SHOWING ME YOUR
FACE THROUGH THE PEOPLE WHO LOVE ME.

Tell the World

Give thanks to the Lord and proclaim his greatness.
Let the whole world know what he has done.

1 Chronicles 16:8 nlt

When we're truly excited about something, we can hardly keep silent about it. Thankfulness is a personal feeling, an intimate emotion that we cherish deep in our hearts. It can be a quiet sense of gratitude that we privately return to again and again throughout our days. At the same time, though, thankfulness spills over. It tells the world what God has done. That doesn't mean we need to become obnoxious people who shove our beliefs about God down others' throats. In quiet, sometimes understated ways, though, our gratitude will shine out from us. Through our lives, the whole world will see God's amazing love in action.

GOD, MAY MY LIFE BE AN UNENDING
STORY OF GRATITUDE TO YOU.

The Aroma of God

Thanks be to God, who always leads us in triumph in Christ, and manifests through us the sweet aroma of the knowledge of Him in every place.

2 CORINTHIANS 2:14 NASB

Some of us were brought up in churches where we were encouraged to "witness" to others about the salvation of Christ. Sometimes we got the idea that this witnessing had to be an unnatural sort of thing where we cornered poor hapless souls and hammered the way of salvation into their heads. In this verse, however, Paul is writing about a very different kind of witness. It's not something we do for God; it's something God just naturally does *through* us as we live in a relationship with Him. Everywhere we go, others will breathe the sweet scent of His presence—not because we're shoving it down their throats, but because God is at work through us. Thanks be to God!

DEAR LORD, DRAW ME CLOSER AND
CLOSER TO YOU SO THAT OTHERS
WILL SMELL YOUR SCENT ON ME.

God of Our Ancestors

"I thank and praise you, God of my ancestors:
You have given me wisdom and power."

- - - - - - - - - - - - - - - - - - - -

Genealogists tell us that over twelve generations and four hundred years, it took 4,094 ancestors to lead to the birth of each one of us. Think of all those individuals who suffered and rejoiced, toiled and sacrificed, lived and died! If just one of them had died without bearing children, we would not be here today. But God was with our ancestors back through the generations. He was already blessing us four hundred years ago. . .and four thousand years ago. He did not forsake our ancestors—and He will not forsake us. We have so many reasons to give Him thanks!

GOD OF MY ANCESTORS, I THANK YOU FOR YOUR FAITHFULNESS DOWN THROUGH THE GENERATIONS. MAY I MAKE GOOD USE OF THE FOUNDATION YOU HAVE GIVEN ME AND GROW IN WISDOM AND POWER.

Others' Lives

Dear brothers and sisters, we can't help but thank God for you, because your faith is flourishing and your love for one another is growing.

2 THESSALONIANS 1:3 NLT

God has given us many reasons to be thankful. Each of our lives overflows with blessings, even in the midst of troubles and suffering. But have you ever considered thanking God for all that He is doing in others' lives? Look at the lives of your children, your spouse, your extended family, and your friends. Pay attention to what God is doing in and through them. As you notice their faith flourish and their love grow, you can affirm God's working within their lives, giving them encouragement and new strength—and you'll also have one more reason to offer up gratitude to God.

THANK YOU, DEAR LORD, FOR ALL YOU ARE DOING IN MY LOVED ONES' LIVES. I SEE YOUR HAND AT WORK, AND I PRAISE YOU.

Helping Others

Carrying out this social relief work involves far more than helping meet the bare needs of poor Christians. It also produces abundant and bountiful thanksgivings to God. This relief offering is a prod to live at your very best, showing your gratitude to God by being openly obedient to the plain meaning of the Message of Christ. You show your gratitude through your generous offerings to your needy brothers and sisters, and really toward everyone.

2 CORINTHIANS 9:12–13 MSG

The Bible makes clear that we are to be concerned not only with the souls of others but also with their physical well-being. As we reach out in practical ways to those who are in need, whether emotionally or physically, we not only help them, but we also express our gratitude to God for all He has done in our own lives. We become part of an ever-growing network of love that spreads abundance and thanksgiving from our lives out into the world.

LORD, SHOW ME WHERE AND HOW I CAN
BE OF SERVICE TO THOSE IN NEED.

Celestial Thanksgiving

And all the angels stood round about the throne. . .and
fell before the throne on their faces, and worshipped
God, saying, Amen: Blessing, and glory, and wisdom,
and thanksgiving, and honour, and power, and
might, be unto our God for ever and ever. Amen.

REVELATION 7:11–12 KJV

Over and over again throughout the Bible, we are reminded to be filled with gratitude, to offer up thanksgiving to the God who has blessed us so richly. But gratitude is not only a human characteristic that draws us closer to God; it is also something that flows through all creation. When John had his amazing revelation of heaven, he saw the angels there falling on their faces and singing songs of thanksgiving. So when we too lift our voices in gratitude to God for all He has done, we are joining in the angels' song! We are becoming part of heaven's endless anthem of praise.

REMIND ME, FATHER GOD, THAT WHEN
I GIVE YOU THANKS, I AM JOINING
MY HEART WITH THE ANGELS.

Our Work for the Lord

I thank Christ Jesus our Lord, who has given me strength to do his work. He considered me trustworthy and appointed me to serve him.

1 TIMOTHY 1:12 NLT

- -

God calls each of us to some work. That God-given work may find its expression in our careers, the jobs that pay us money, but it may also extend far beyond our nine-to-five employment. This work is uniquely suited to each of us; no one else could do it as well or the same. It is one of the reasons God created us, and it is meant to give us as much joy as it does others. Whether it's cooking meals for those who need them, lending a listening ear to those who are troubled, writing grant proposals for a nonprofit organization in need of funds, helping people with their taxes, or painting beautiful images, God uses our work to build His kingdom.

CHRIST JESUS, HELP ME TO REMEMBER THAT THE WORK YOU HAVE GIVEN ME IS ONE MORE REASON FOR ME TO THANK YOU.

Shaky Times

*Therefore, since we are receiving a kingdom that
cannot be shaken, let us be thankful, and so worship
God acceptably with reverence and awe.*

HEBREWS 12:28 NIV

We live in a shaky world. Pandemics, protests, and politics have made all of us feel a little wobbly. We fret about what will happen next. We worry about our children and other loved ones. Often we feel helpless and anxious, maybe even terrified at times. But even though our world has its share of financial, societal, and spiritual earthquakes, we need to remember that we also inhabit the kingdom of God—and *that* kingdom can never be shaken. No matter what happens in the world, we can continue to be thankful and at peace, knowing we are truly citizens of another world, one that is unshakable.

THANK YOU, LORD GOD, THAT NO MATTER
WHAT HAPPENS, I AM SAFE IN YOU.

Past, Present, and Future

We give thee thanks, O LORD God Almighty,
which art, and wast, and art to come.

REVELATION 11:17 KJV

Psychologists have noted that the human brain has a hard time resting in the present moment. Instead, we tend to either obsess about the past or drive ourselves crazy worrying about the future. God wants to meet us right here, in this present moment, and we may miss out on what He is doing *now* when we are preoccupied by the past or the future. But we can rest assured that whether our minds are focused on the past, the present, or the future, God is right there. We can thank Him that He is a past, present, and future God.

LORD GOD ALMIGHTY, THANK YOU THAT YOU WERE THERE IN MY PAST; THANK YOU THAT YOU ARE HERE IN THIS PRESENT MOMENT; AND THANK YOU THAT YOU WILL BE WITH ME IN THE FUTURE, ALL THE WAY TO ETERNITY.

Big Enough

Out of them shall proceed thanksgiving and the voice of them that make merry: and I will multiply them, and they shall not be few; I will also glorify them, and they shall not be small.

JEREMIAH 30:19 KJV

Do you ever feel small? Even though we are grown-ups with adult responsibilities, most of us have at least a little piece inside us that never quite grew up. That inner child can be a source of joy and fun but also can make us feel too little to cope with life's challenges. God wants to bless that child, though, and one of the ways we allow Him to do that is by making gratitude a habit. As we practice thanksgiving daily, He fills us with light. We will still be able to laugh and play like a child—"make merry," as the King James Version says—but we will also be big enough to take on the work God has ordained for us.

THANK YOU, GOD, THAT YOUR LOVE LIFTS ME UP, STRENGTHENS ME, AND MAKES ME BIG ENOUGH TO FACE THE CHALLENGES OF MY LIFE.

Spilling Over

Our prayers for you are always spilling over into thanksgivings. We can't quit thanking God our Father and Jesus our Messiah for you!

COLOSSIANS 1:3 MSG

The Bible tells us to pray for one another. As we lift up one another's troubles and trials to God, we join in God's work of love and empowerment. But we need not let our hearts be weighed down by others' pain and problems. Instead, our prayers can spill over into thanksgiving. We can be filled with expectation and hope, for although we don't know how God will answer our prayers, we do know that He *will*. God will do something amazing and marvelous in the lives of those we love—and gratitude affirms that reality.

THANK YOU, LORD, FOR ALL YOU ARE DOING IN THE LIVES OF THOSE I LOVE.

United

I will give You thanks in the great congregation;
I will praise You among a mighty throng.

Gratitude is a private, personal emotion. We experience it as individuals. But we can give expression to it in unity with others. Whether at church or in some other group that is doing God's work, when we lift our hearts and voices with others, we will find that we are strengthened and encouraged. Our own heart's thanksgiving expands and joins with others' praise. It's a little like singing: one voice alone is beautiful, but a chorus of many voices can make us feel as though we are experiencing a little bit of heaven!

I THANK YOU, LORD, FOR OPPORTUNITIES TO LIFT MY VOICE IN THANKSGIVING, UNITED WITH OTHER VOICES THAT ARE ALSO PRAISING YOU.

Sleepless Nights

At midnight I rise to give you thanks.

PSALM 119:62 NIV

We may not want to set our alarms to wake us in the middle of the night for a prayer session with God (though it might not be a bad idea to do that from time to time!), but there are nights that find us lying awake as the minutes and then hours tick past. When sleep won't come, it's easy to find ourselves going over all our worries, magnifying them until they loom over us and our hearts beat faster with anxiety. But we have other options. On those nights when insomnia overtakes us, we can use the wakeful hours to turn to God in gratitude. Instead of counting sheep, we can count our blessings—and as thanksgiving fills our hearts, we may find ourselves relaxing into sleep.

LORD, WHEN SLEEP WON'T COME,
REMIND ME TO TURN MY WORRIES INTO
THANKSGIVING FOR ALL YOUR BLESSINGS.

Repetition

Give thanks to the LORD, for he is good! His faithful love endures forever. Give thanks to the God of gods. His faithful love endures forever. Give thanks to the Lord of lords. His faithful love endures forever. Give thanks to him who alone does mighty miracles. His faithful love endures forever. Give thanks to him who made the heavens so skillfully. His faithful love endures forever. . . . Give thanks to the God of heaven. His faithful love endures forever.

PSALM 136:1–5, 26 NLT

The psalmist knew the secret of gratitude. He understood that thanksgiving never gets boring, no matter how many times it's repeated. In fact, with each expression of gratitude, our hearts expand, allowing God's Spirit to fill us ever more deeply. These verses from Psalm 136 are good ones to repeat throughout the day, reminding us of God's faithful love that will endure forever.

YOU ARE SO GOOD, LORD. YOUR
FAITHFUL LOVE ENDURES FOREVER.

Praying for Everyone

I urge you, first of all, to pray for all people. Ask God to help
them; intercede on their behalf, and give thanks for them.

1 TIMOTHY 2:1 NLT

Most of us pray for the people who are important to us, our family
and friends we love so much—but in this verse, the Bible is telling us
to pray for *all* people. That includes people we don't know personally,
such as people we've heard about in the news. Whenever we read or
watch a news story, we can make a habit of saying a prayer for the
individuals concerned. The instruction to pray for all people also
includes people we don't like. It includes people who do bad things.
And not only are we told to lift them up to God, asking that He would
bless them and help them, but we are also told to give thanks for them.
This is the radical gratitude that reaches out beyond our selfishness
and embraces the entire world.

JESUS, FRIEND OF ALL HUMANITY, TEACH ME
TO LOVE AS YOU LOVE. MAY MY PRAYERS OF
INTERCESSION AND GRATITUDE NOT ONLY BLESS
OTHERS BUT ALSO DRAW ME EVER CLOSER TO YOU.

Living Our Faith

You know your way around the faith. Now do what you've been taught. School's out; quit studying the subject and start living it! And let your living spill over into thanksgiving.
COLOSSIANS 2:7 MSG

Here it is again: the Bible is telling us that thanksgiving is essential to following Jesus. If we want to practice what we preach—or practice what has been preached to us—then it's time for us to start living our faith, allowing our beliefs to become visible in the way we interact with the world around us. Doing that should just naturally spill over into gratitude to God for all He does for us. Believing, living, thanking becomes an ongoing cycle that will bless not only our own hearts and lives but everyone whose lives we touch. Thanksgiving is like the body's circulation system, necessary for the ongoing life of our spirits.

LORD, I WANT TO WALK THE TALK. AND I WANT GRATITUDE TO FLOW THROUGH ME, CARRYING YOUR SPIRIT TO EACH ASPECT OF MY LIFE.

God's Name

We give thanks to You, O God, we give thanks, for Your name is near.

PSALM 75:1 NASB

Sometimes we feel as though God is far away. He doesn't seem to have much to do with the details of our daily lives; He seems distant from the chaos of world affairs. This verse from Psalms reminds us, though, that God's name is as close to us as our own. It is always there, available for us to call on. All we need to do is call out God's name—and He will answer us. Maybe not always in the way we expect or hope, but nevertheless, God reveals His presence to us in His answers to prayer. We can give thanks even while we're still praying, as we cry out His name, because we can be confident that He will answer.

I'M CALLING OUT YOUR NAME, LORD GOD.
THANK YOU THAT YOU HEAR ME.

Thanksgiving in the Lions' Den

When Daniel learned that the document had been signed, he went into his house. The windows in its upper room opened toward Jerusalem, and three times a day he got down on his knees, prayed, and gave thanks to his God, just as he had done before.

DANIEL 6:10 HCSB

This verse gives us a little glimpse into the life of Daniel. This document that had been signed meant that a law had been passed forbidding the people in the kingdom to pray to anyone but King Darius. It meant trouble for Daniel—but he didn't let it change his behavior. He continued to pray to his God just as he always had. And even knowing that his life was now in danger, he still gave thanks to God. He knew that the God he served was King of the entire universe, and no matter what happened, he trusted God to make all things right. Daniel ended up in the lions' den, but the lions didn't eat him. His God protected him.

> LORD, WHEN I FIND MYSELF IN A "LIONS' DEN" OF TROUBLE, HELP ME NOT ONLY TO TRUST YOU, AS DANIEL DID; HELP ME ALSO TO THANK YOU FOR THE WORK YOU WILL DO EVEN THERE, IN MY TIME OF DANGER.

All Humanity

Let them give thanks to the LORD for His faithful love and His wonderful works for all humanity. For He has satisfied the thirsty and filled the hungry with good things.

PSALM 107:8–9 HCSB

Sometimes it's easy to see only the piece of the world that's in front of our noses. We forget how immense the earth is and how many different kinds of people live around the globe. The problems and suffering of those who live on another continent may not seem very real to us, but God does not forget any human being. Each one is real and treasured. He faithfully loves all humanity, and He blesses each person in the way they most need. We can try to catch a glimpse from the divine perspective and perceive all of our planet's inhabitants as one united family, despite our differences. When we do, may our hearts spill over with gratitude for all the ways that God finds to bless the human race.

WIDEN MY PERSPECTIVE, LORD, SO THAT I MAY EXPERIENCE THE LOVE YOU HAVE FOR ALL HUMANITY.

Blessing God

Bless the LORD, O my soul, and forget none of His benefits.

PSALM 103:2 NASB

- -

At first glance, this verse may seem a little odd. Why would God need *us* to bless *Him*? Shouldn't it be the other way around? The original Hebrew word used here, though, meant "to kneel down, to thank, to praise." This is how we bless God—by surrendering ourselves to Him, thanking Him, and praising Him. We stop overlooking all He has done for us, and we offer our gratitude for each of the blessings (the benefits) He has bestowed on us, even the small, everyday ones. When we do this, we create a cycle of blessing that flows from our hearts to God's and back again.

I WANT TO BLESS YOU, LORD, AS YOU HAVE SO
RICHLY BLESSED ME. SO I'M COMING TO YOU,
THANKING YOU FOR ALL YOU HAVE DONE FOR ME.

A State of Gratitude

Jesus then took the loaves, gave thanks, and distributed to those who were seated as much as they wanted. He did the same with the fish.

JOHN 6:11 NIV

In this verse, Jesus is modeling for us how we are to behave when we receive a gift, no matter how small. A crowd of hungry people surrounded Jesus, and the only food anyone had offered to share was a small boy's lunch. But Jesus did not dismiss the gift as being so meager as to be useless. Instead, the original language in which this account was written reports that Jesus was in a "state of gratitude." He was thankful for what had been given to Him, even though it was small—and then He shared it with everyone else gathered around Him. When we too learn to be thankful for even the smallest gifts, when we learn to share what we have been given with others, who knows how God may choose to bless us?

JESUS, TEACH ME TO BE MORE LIKE YOU. MAY I LEARN TO LIVE MY LIFE IN A STATE OF GRATITUDE.

No Outsiders

One of them, when he saw he was healed, came back, praising God in a loud voice. He threw himself at Jesus' feet and thanked him—and he was a Samaritan. Jesus asked, "Were not all ten cleansed? Where are the other nine? Has no one returned to give praise to God except this foreigner?" Then he said to him, "Rise and go; your faith has made you well."

LUKE 17:15–19 NIV

In Jesus' day, Jews considered Samaritans to be outsiders. They were scorned, thought to be less worthy than Jews. They were also thought to be dangerous, the sort of people good Jews tried to avoid. In the story of the ten lepers, Jesus makes clear that His blessings are for all people, not just the people who look like us, speak like us, or worship God like us. It may even be that the people we consider "outsiders" have a deeper grasp of God than we do. We may need to open our hearts so that we can learn about thankfulness and humility from those who understand these qualities better than we do.

SHOW ME, JESUS, ANY SECRET PREJUDICES I'VE HIDDEN IN MY HEART. MAKE MY HEART HUMBLE ENOUGH TO BE OPEN AND GRATEFUL ENOUGH TO NEVER FORGET TO THANK YOU.

Eating

Whoever eats meat does so to the Lord, for they give thanks to God; and whoever abstains does so to the Lord and gives thanks to God.

ROMANS 14:6 NIV

We live in a culture that is constantly telling us to diet. "Eat less so you'll be thin" is the message everywhere we turn. "Follow this special diet, and you'll lose that weight that's keeping you from being attractive." That message is hard to resist, and it makes our relationship with food complicated. God does want us to be healthy, and the Bible says that gluttony is a sin against the body, just as much as any other unhealthy habit. But this verse from the book of Romans reminds us that God wants to heal our relationship with food. If He has called us to reduce our calories, we can do so with thanksgiving—and when we eat, we can also do so with thanksgiving.

FATHER GOD, HEAL MY RELATIONSHIP WITH FOOD. SHOW ME WHAT IS HEALTHY FOR ME, AND MAY I ALWAYS EAT WITH GRATITUDE THAT YOU HAVE GIVEN ME ENOUGH.

Newcomers

You and the Levites and the foreigners residing among you shall rejoice in all the good things the LORD your God has given to you and your household.

DEUTERONOMY 26:11 NIV

- -

The Bible makes clear that our attitude toward strangers and newcomers must always be one of welcome and acceptance. In this verse, the Bible is telling us that we have more in common with these people than we may think. God has blessed all of us, and we can unite our hearts in gratitude. We don't need to be afraid that there won't be enough to go around, because God will supply. He will take care of our individual households—and as we trust Him to do that, we can lift our hearts in thanksgiving and generosity with those who are new to our communities. Thanksgiving is the antidote to fear and distrust.

LORD GOD, GIVE ME A GRATEFUL HEART THAT ISN'T AFRAID TO WELCOME NEWCOMERS.

Great Things and Small

The LORD has done great things for us; we are glad.

PSALM 126:3 NASB

What makes you happy? It might be a sunny day after a week of clouds. It could be good news from a loved one. It might be something as small as a new outfit, a good hair day, or the way a friend makes you laugh. Whatever it is, big or small, God wants us to share it with Him. He doesn't want us to keep our happiness to ourselves. He wants us to remember that everything comes from His hand. The Lord has done great things for us—and He has done countless small things as well. His love is strewn through our lives. As we learn to practice gratitude, our hearts will fill up with gladness, and the gladness can then in turn fuel our gratitude, a continual cycle of joy and thanksgiving.

THANK YOU, LORD, FOR ALL YOU GIVE TO
ME, FOR BLESSINGS BIG AND SMALL.

Competition and Envy

Isn't everything you have and everything you are sheer gifts from God? So what's the point of all this comparing and competing?

1 CORINTHIANS 4:7 MSG

Do you ever find yourself comparing your life to others' lives? Maybe you wonder why a colleague got a raise or a promotion when you didn't. Or you wish your body was as thin and fit as your friend's. Perhaps you envy the number of friends a family member has compared to your own smaller circle. Envy can be a repetitive small twinge that jabs at our contentment—or it can grow into an all-consuming jealousy that saps the joy from our lives. Either way, it interferes with our practice of gratitude. Envy and jealousy and competition say, in effect, that what God has given me isn't *enough*. But God always gives us exactly what we need. We don't need to compare ourselves to others because He treats us each as individuals, giving us exactly what is best.

LORD, MAY I TRUST YOU ENOUGH, MAY MY GRATITUDE BE SO GREAT, THAT THERE'S NO ROOM IN MY LIFE FOR COMPETITION AND ENVY.

Cultivating Thankfulness

*Let the peace of Christ keep you in tune with each other,
in step with each other. None of this going off and doing
your own thing. And cultivate thankfulness. Let the Word
of Christ—the Message—have the run of the house.*

COLOSSIANS 3:15 MSG

Yet again the Bible is pointing out how important gratitude is as a spiritual practice. The implication here is that thankfulness will act as a bond that helps us to keep in step with others (rather than arguing and being in competition). Gratitude opens the doors of our hearts to one another—and it opens our hearts to Christ as well. It makes space in us for the Word to have a say in our inner beings as well as our entire lives. This verse also says that we have control over how much gratitude is in our lives. We can "cultivate" it, actively planting the seeds of thanksgiving and consciously and constantly watering them until they grow.

TEACH ME, LORD JESUS, TO CULTIVATE
THANKFULNESS AS MY CONSTANT
SPIRITUAL PRACTICE.

Humble Gratitude

*Therefore if there is any encouragement in Christ, if there is
any consolation of love, if there is any fellowship of the Spirit,
if any affection and compassion, make my joy complete by
being of the same mind, maintaining the same love, united in
spirit, intent on one purpose. Do nothing from selfishness or
empty conceit, but with humility of mind regard one another
as more important than yourselves; do not merely look out for
your own personal interests, but also for the interests of others.
Have this attitude in yourselves which was also in Christ Jesus.*

PHILIPPIANS 2:1–5 NASB

Gratitude and pride don't walk together. Pride says, "I don't need to
say thank you for anything." It says, "I worry about myself first and
foremost." Pride separates us from others. It builds walls. Gratitude,
on the other hand, says, "I owe everything to God." It looks for opportunities to say thank you, both to God and to others. It draws us
closer to one another and to the Lord. It makes us more like Jesus.

JESUS, I WANT TO BE LIKE YOU. MAY GRATITUDE
DRIVE PRIDE OUT OF MY HEART.

Encouraging One Another

And let us not neglect our meeting together,
as some people do, but encourage one another.
HEBREWS 10:25 NLT

It's not always easy to practice gratitude. When things are going "our way," we may find that gratitude comes more naturally to us, but when everything seems to be going wrong, whether our lives are falling apart in big ways or small irritations are accumulating, then thanksgiving becomes harder to practice. When we find ourselves struggling with gratitude, it's good to be able to get encouragement from others. We don't have to do life alone. In fact, the Bible tells us repeatedly that the spiritual life is healthier and easier when it's done in community. So when gratitude becomes hard, lean on others—and then allow others to lean on you when the shoe is on the other foot.

THANK YOU, JESUS, FOR YOUR BODY, THE COMMUNITY OF FAITH. MAY I NEVER SEPARATE MYSELF FROM OTHERS WHO ARE FOLLOWING YOU.

Ungratefulness

People will be lovers of themselves, lovers of money, boastful, proud, abusive, disobedient to their parents, ungrateful, unholy, without love, unforgiving, slanderous, without self-control, brutal, not lovers of the good, treacherous, rash, conceited, lovers of pleasure rather than lovers of God—having a form of godliness but denying its power.

2 TIMOTHY 3:2–5 NIV

The Bible rates the opposite of being thankful—being ungrateful—as just as dangerous as being selfish, greedy, gossipy, hateful, and abusive. People without gratitude may look godly and spiritual from the outside, but they lack the true inner power that the love of God gives to us. If we turn this verse around and look at the positive attributes, we see that being thankful goes along with being unselfish, generous, humble, gentle, respectful of parents, holy, loving, forgiving, kind, self-controlled, lovers of goodness, trustworthy, careful, and lovers of God. People like this have true spiritual power.

LORD, MAY MY LOVE FOR YOU BE TRUE,
FILLED WITH GRATITUDE AND ALL THE OTHER
VIRTUES THAT GO ALONG WITH IT.

Grace-Full

For by grace you have been saved through faith;
and that not of yourselves, it is the gift of God;
not as a result of works, so that no one may boast.

EPHESIANS 2:8–9 NASB

The original Greek word that our Bibles translate as "grace" included gratitude within its meaning. It meant not only that God has freely granted to us His love and blessings, but also that as a result of God's grace, we become "grace-full," which in the original language meant "thankful, grateful." It's one of those reciprocal cycles that are so common in God's kingdom: first God grants us His grace; then we respond with gratitude, which makes us even more full of grace; and then God continues to pour out His grace on us as we continue to respond with thanksgiving.

LORD, MAY I BECOME EVER MORE FULL
OF GRACE AND GRATITUDE.

The Proper Vantage Point

"My grace is all you need. My power works best in weakness." So now I am glad to boast about my weaknesses, so that the power of Christ can work through me.

2 CORINTHIANS 12:9 NLT

So often we feel as though we're not enough. Not smart enough, not talented enough, not popular enough, not attractive enough. . .the list can go on and on. But God reminds us that His grace is all we need. Where we are "not enough," He is more than enough! The word used in this verse—"boast"—meant, according to HELPS Word-Studies, to "live with the head up high"; to "have the particular vantage point, the right base of operation"; "to deal successfully with a matter." Gratitude gives us the right vantage point. It allows God to make us strong through our weaknesses.

HELP ME, LORD JESUS, TO SEE THINGS
FROM YOUR VANTAGE POINT SO THAT
I MAY ALWAYS BOAST IN YOU.

Serving God

If by grace, then is it no more of works: otherwise grace is no more grace. But if it be of works, then it is no more grace.

ROMANS 11:6 KJV

God calls us to serve Him by carrying out actions of love for others, by giving what we have to those who have less, and by working to build His kingdom here on earth. But we never earn God's love by performing acts of justice and kindness, for God's love is already ours, unconditionally. That is what grace is. And that is why we give all our thanks to God. If we had earned His love and blessings by working hard, we wouldn't need to feel grateful—but since God gives to us freely, regardless of our actions, our hearts overflow with gratitude.

BECAUSE I AM SO GRATEFUL FOR YOUR FREELY GIVEN GRACE, LORD, I WANT TO SERVE YOU.

Pride

He gives grace generously. As the Scriptures say,
"God opposes the proud but gives grace to the humble."

JAMES 4:6 NLT

- -

Grace is what God gives us, and gratitude is what we give back to God in return. Gratitude makes more room in our lives for God's grace, and God's grace makes us ever more grateful. Pride, however, blocks this circular flow that would otherwise proceed naturally from God's heart to ours. Humility, grace, and gratitude accompany one another, but arrogance—the kind of pride that says, "I'm better than everyone else"—interferes with God's generosity. Pride says, "I already have everything I need," and as a result, no room is left for God's gifts. Humility, however, leads to gratitude, which leads to grace!

SHOW ME, LORD, WHEN I AM FULL OF DESTRUCTIVE PRIDE. I DON'T WANT TO BLOCK THE FLOW OF YOUR GRACE.

Our Abundant God

We have all received grace after grace from His fullness.
JOHN 1:16 HCSB

Our God is not a stingy God, nor does He lack resources from which to draw. No, God is full, abundant, overflowing, and He shares all that He is with limitless generosity. We have so many reasons to be grateful, for He has given us "grace after grace." He blesses us daily with physical blessings—but even more, He also piles spiritual blessings onto our souls. When we have eyes to see, we realize that everywhere we turn, God is there, blessing us, pouring out His generous grace in more ways than we could possibly imagine.

THANK YOU, LORD, THAT YOU ARE
SUCH AN ABUNDANT GOD!

A Thousand Generations

"God, a God of mercy and grace, endlessly patient—so much love, so deeply true—loyal in love for a thousand generations, forgiving iniquity, rebellion, and sin."

EXODUS 34:6 MSG

What an amazing God we have. This verse seems to say it all: God is full of mercy and kindness; He doesn't treat us the way we "deserve" but instead is endlessly patient with our mistakes and failures. His love is so deep, so loyal, so true, that it stretches back a thousand generations. Long, long ago, God was already loving us, already planning to bless us, already forgiving us for our rebellion against Him, already planning to heal us and make us whole. No wonder our hearts spill over with gratitude!

I CAN'T BEGIN TO GRASP YOUR LOVE, LORD. IT FILLS ME WITH AWE AND A DEEP, DEEP GRATITUDE THAT GOES DOWN TO THE ROOTS OF MY BEING.

Polarization

*That you may learn from us. . .that none of you will be
inflated with pride in favor of one person over another.*
1 CORINTHIANS 4:6 HCSB

When Paul wrote this to the church at Corinth, the people there were
having a problem with partisanship. Some of them followed Paul;
others followed Peter. That would have been fine if both groups had
respected each other, but instead, they became rivals. The community was polarized between Paul followers and Peter followers. The
situation was actually a lot like what we face in our country today,
where so many people have allowed politics to become a source of
pride and division. "Learn from both of us," Paul says. "Be humble.
Make room for others' opinions and treat them with respect. Stop
being so full of certainty that you're the only one who's right. Create
space for humility and gratitude."

I THANK YOU, GOD, THAT YOU UNDERSTAND
OUR COMPLICATED WORLD. MAY GRATITUDE
AND HUMILITY OPEN UP MY HEART TO THOSE
WHO THINK DIFFERENTLY THAN ME.

True

"God's grace and truth go with you!"
2 SAMUEL 15:20 MSG

We are grateful for God's grace, but why do we need His truth? What is the Bible saying here? Maybe we need God's truth because in a world where so much is false, we can count on God to always be real. Other versions of the Bible translate "truth" as "faithfulness," and the original Hebrew word used here meant "reliability, steadiness, certainty, continuity," as well as "true." Think about it: Lies don't last; sooner or later they are exposed. Lies can't be depended on; sooner or later they let us down. Lies are shaky ground on which to build our lives. We can be grateful that our God is reliable, steady, faithful—and true.

LORD, I THANK YOU THAT YOU ARE THE TRUTH AT THE CENTER OF MY LIFE, THE STEADY ROCK UNDER MY FEET.

Sheer Generosity

*Out of sheer generosity he put us in right standing
with himself. A pure gift. He got us out of the mess
we're in and restored us to where he always wanted
us to be. And he did it by means of Jesus Christ.*

ROMANS 3:24 MSG

- -

We are grateful when someone gives us a birthday or Christmas gift, but we are even more thankful when someone surprises us with a present out of the blue, for no particular occasion or reason. That's sheer generosity, with no sense of obligation involved. Jesus is God's gift to us, a gift He didn't have to give, that He was under no obligation to offer, and yet He did. Through Jesus, we find ourselves lifted out of our failures and mistakes. Through this most amazing of gifts, we are drawn close to God and wrapped in His love. How can we respond to such generosity except with hearts full of gratitude?

THANK YOU, JESUS, FOR THE GIFT OF YOURSELF.

Overflowing Grace

God is able to make every grace overflow to you,
so that in every way, always having everything
you need, you may excel in every good work.

2 CORINTHIANS 9:8 HCSB

Do you ever feel as though you don't have enough of what you need? Maybe you don't think you have enough money, or maybe you don't believe you're talented enough or intelligent enough to do a job that you've been given. When you have those feelings of inadequacy, turn them into gratitude—for God has promised to give you not only everything you need, but even *more* than you need, so that you can excel in the work of His kingdom.

THANK YOU, JESUS, THAT YOUR
GRACE OVERFLOWS.

Growing in Grace

Grow in grace, and in the knowledge of our
Lord and Saviour Jesus Christ.
2 PETER 3:18 KJV

If grace is a gift from God, how does it make sense that we can *grow in grace*? What did the apostle Peter mean when he wrote these words? Perhaps he understood that gratitude is the other side of grace—and the more gratitude we feel toward God, the more we open ourselves to greater grace. Peter gives us a clue to what he means in this verse: he indicates that as we get to know Jesus better, we will also grow in grace. Gratitude opens our hearts to a deeper relationship with Jesus, and grace pours out from the relationship. This is the way we grow spiritually; this is the way we grow into the people God created us to be.

I WANT TO GET TO KNOW YOU BETTER, JESUS. I AM
SO GRATEFUL FOR ALL YOU HAVE DONE FOR ME.

Strong, Firm, and Steadfast

*The God of all grace, who called you to his eternal glory in
Christ, after you have suffered a little while, will himself
restore you and make you strong, firm and steadfast.*

1 PETER 5:10 NIV

Following Jesus doesn't mean we never experience hard times. The Bible is clear about this. And no matter how spiritually mature we are, we will always encounter times of doubt and suffering. But even in the midst of those painful times, we can still be grateful. The God of grace—the God who gives to us so freely and unconditionally—will never abandon us to the hard moments of our lives. He won't leave us there. In His good time, He will reach down and restore us, healing our doubts and comforting our pain, so that we are once more strong, firm, and steadfast.

REMIND ME, LORD, TO BE GRATEFUL IN THE HARD
TIMES, CONFIDENT THAT YOU WILL RESCUE ME.

Bitter Roots

*See to it that no one comes short of the grace of God;
that no root of bitterness springing up causes trouble.*

HEBREWS 12:15 NASB

God's grace is unconditional—but we have the power to cut ourselves off from it. This verse speaks of a "root of bitterness" that can cause us to "come short" of God's grace. In the Greek, the word our Bibles have translated as "come short" meant "to come late, causing a lack." God is pouring out His grace, but we fail to show up on time to receive it. As a result, we don't have everything we need, all because we let bitterness (resentment, jealousy, and hatred, for example) take root in our hearts. How do we pull out that root? With gratitude. Turning to God with a thankful heart leaves no more room for bitterness to grow.

I ASK YOU, LORD, TO PULL OUT BY THE ROOTS
ANY BITTERNESS GROWING IN MY HEART. MAY
MY GRATITUDE FOR ALL YOU HAVE DONE FOR
ME MAKE MORE ROOM FOR YOUR GRACE.

Immense and Incredible

Immense in mercy and with an incredible love, he embraced us. He took our sin-dead lives and made us alive in Christ. He did all this on his own, with no help from us! Then he picked us up and set us down in highest heaven in company with Jesus, our Messiah.

EPHESIANS 2:4–6 MSG

- -

We have so many reasons to feel gratitude. These verses that Paul wrote to the church at Ephesus summarize some of the biggest things God has done for us. First, God embraced us; the Creator of the universe felt such incredible love for us, such immense mercy, that He reached out to hug us tight. Then, through Christ, He brought back to life everything in us that was dead—and He did it all on His own initiative, with no effort on our part. And *then*, as if that wasn't enough, He picked us up and placed us in heaven, with Jesus to keep us company there. The next time you have a hard time feeling grateful for much of anything, think about *that*.

FATHER, THANK YOU FOR EMBRACING ME WITH YOUR ALL-ENCOMPASSING LOVE. MY HEART IS OVERFLOWING WITH GRATITUDE TODAY.

Humble Clothes

All of you clothe yourselves with humility toward one another,
because God resists the proud but gives grace to the humble.
1 PETER 5:5 HCSB

Once again we have the Bible's formula for spiritual happiness and growth: humility + gratitude = God's grace. Grace and gratitude reflect each other, and both find their place in our hearts when we live lives of humility rather than pride. And yet it's so easy sometimes to interact with others from a place of pride. We fear being hurt; we worry that people will think we're silly or look down on us. But the apostle Peter is telling us here that we don't need to erect a shield of pride around our heart for protection. Instead, we can clothe ourselves with humility. This is soft and gentle clothing that allows others to come close to us. It allows God's grace to soak into our hearts.

REMIND ME, JESUS, TO CLOTHE MYSELF IN THE
SAME HUMILITY THAT YOU WORE. MAY I ALWAYS
BE HUMBLE ENOUGH TO BE GRATEFUL.

Reason To Be Grateful

God, who set me apart from my mother's womb and called me by his grace, was pleased to reveal his Son in me.

GALATIANS 1:15–16 NIV

Sometimes it's hard to see much reason for gratitude. The troubles in our lives can loom so large and dark that we have trouble perceiving God's grace. In times like that, it's good to reread Bible verses that remind us of all God has done for us. We were loved as individuals before we were even born. God has a particular plan for each one of us. And God reveals Christ to the world through each of us uniquely. That knowledge is humbling—and it's a good reason to feel grateful, even in the midst of life's darkness and difficulties.

THANK YOU, GOD, FOR LOVING ME, FOR CALLING ME, FOR USING ME IN YOUR KINGDOM.

True Wealth

Tell those rich in this world's wealth to quit being so full of themselves and so obsessed with money, which is here today and gone tomorrow. Tell them to go after God, who piles on all the riches we could ever manage—to do good, to be rich in helping others, to be extravagantly generous.

1 TIMOTHY 6:17–18 MSG

If we've been given material blessings in the form of financial security, then we can feel grateful for God's provision, but we also need to remember that money is always only a temporary blessing. It comes and it goes—and we cannot take it with us when we leave this world. These verses tell us to focus on a different sort of riches: the spiritual wealth of being able to help others, of being able to give generously. When we do, we participate in God's free-flowing grace. That's a form of wealth that is eternal. And it's good reason to be truly grateful.

LORD, THANK YOU THAT I HAVE THE PRIVILEGE OF BEING USED BY YOU TO BLESS OTHERS.

Don't Forget!

Praise the LORD, my soul; all my inmost being, praise his holy name. Praise the LORD, my soul, and forget not all his benefits—who forgives all your sins and heals all your diseases, who redeems your life from the pit and crowns you with love and compassion, who satisfies your desires with good things so that your youth is renewed like the eagle's.

PSALM 103:1–5 NIV

Our God is endlessly good to us, but the psalmist understood that sometimes our souls need to be reminded of everything God does. He forgives our sins; He heals us; He redeems us; He honors us with His love and compassion; He satisfies the desires of our hearts; and He renews our spirits so that even in old age they rise up like an eagle's. When our souls remember all these blessings, they brim over with praise and thanks. Gratitude sinks down into our innermost being—and then it spills over into our entire lives.

I AM SO GRATEFUL, GOD, FOR EVERYTHING YOU HAVE DONE FOR ME.

Undeserved

Christ has brought us into this place of undeserved privilege where we now stand, and we confidently and joyfully look forward to sharing God's glory.
ROMANS 5:2 NLT

- - - - - - - - - - - - - - - - - - - -

Through Christ, we have an intimate relationship with God. The Creator of the universe considers us to be just as much His children as Jesus is. That means that Jesus is our Brother. We can look forward to an eternity of sharing God's light and life with Jesus, beginning now and never ending.

We didn't do anything to earn the privilege of being God's children. Christ did it for us, simply because He loved us. All we have to do is say, "Thank You."

FATHER GOD, I AM SO GRATEFUL TO BE YOUR CHILD.

Gratitude versus Negativity

For if by the one man's trespass the many died, how much more have the grace of God and the gift overflowed to the many by the grace of the one man, Jesus Christ.

ROMANS 5:15 HCSB

We live in a world of negativity. The news we hear on the radio and see online and on TV focuses on tragedies and controversies. The Facebook posts that come up on our feed often seem geared to incite feelings of anger and despair. The Bible agrees that sin is a very real problem in the world—but scripture is not negative. Yes, sin exists, but the grace of God is so much more abundant than any darkness our world offers. Genesis tells the story of how death and sin entered the world through Adam, but the Gospels tell the story of God's grace through another man, Jesus Christ. Through Him we can turn away from negativity and despair and instead focus on our gratitude for God's overflowing grace.

THANK YOU, JESUS, THAT YOU ARE THE
ANSWER TO THE WORLD'S NEGATIVITY.

Guilt

Because of his grace he made us right in his sight and gave us confidence that we will inherit eternal life.

TITUS 3:7 NLT

Carrying around guilt on our shoulders is a terrible feeling. It can lead to depression and fear. It leaves no room for gratitude. But God doesn't want us to live our lives in that state. That's why Jesus came, so that we could know we are right with God. We don't have to feel guilty. We don't have to feel sad or scared. Instead, we can be confident that God has set us free from all our failures and mistakes—and through Jesus, we will live with God forever in eternity. When we focus on that reality, our guilt will slip away, leaving only gratitude for all that God has done for us.

I AM SO GRATEFUL, JESUS, THAT BECAUSE OF YOU, I NO LONGER HAVE TO FEEL GUILTY.

Friends

Two people are better off than one,
for they can help each other succeed.
ECCLESIASTES 4:9 NLT

- -

Our friends are gifts from God. Marcel Proust wrote, "Let us be grateful to the people who make us happy; they are the charming gardeners who make our souls blossom." God comes into our lives through the people we know and love. He uses them to help our souls blossom; with the help of another, we can go further, reach higher, and succeed where we otherwise might have failed. This scripture is a reminder not to take our friends for granted—but instead to thank God for them daily, realizing that He uses them to bless us.

THANK YOU FOR THE PEOPLE YOU HAVE PUT IN MY LIFE, LORD. I PRAY THAT I MAY BLESS THEM AS MUCH AS THEY BLESS ME.

Full of Faith and Power

Stephen, full of faith and power, did great
wonders and miracles among the people.

ACTS 6:8 KJV

Sometimes we look at other people and feel amazed by all they accomplish. Next to them, we may even feel a bit inadequate. This verse reminds us, though, that God is the one who gives each of us our gifts. Stephen could do such great works because of his faith in God. We can be grateful for the "Stephens" of the world, and at the same time, we can thank God for the unique gifts He has given to each one of us. We are not all called to be Stephens, doing amazing acts that draw the attention of people. Some of us may be called to work quietly, behind the scenes, our gifts seldom if ever noticed—but no less deserving of gratitude.

GIVE ME THE FAITH AND POWER I NEED, LORD,
TO DO THE WORK TO WHICH YOU HAVE CALLED
ME. HELP ME NEVER TO FORGET TO THANK
YOU FOR WHAT YOU DO THROUGH ME.

Wisdom and Grace

"Prize [wisdom], and she will exalt you; she will honor you if you embrace her. She will place on your head a garland of grace; she will present you with a crown of beauty."

PROVERBS 4:8–9 NASB

- -

These verses summarize once again the reciprocal nature of grace and gratitude. As we honor and embrace wisdom—which the Old Testament describes as being an aspect of God—and as we thank God for all wisdom teaches us and gives to us, we are in return lifted up and crowned, our lives graced with beauty. Wisdom gives us reason to be grateful, and then our gratitude leads to still greater grace, a garland of grace that encircles our entire lives with loveliness, filling our hearts still more with gratitude for wisdom's gifts. When grace is everywhere we turn, how can we help but overflow with thankfulness?

SOURCE OF WISDOM, I HONOR YOU AND EMBRACE YOU; I AM SO GRATEFUL FOR THE GRACE YOU BESTOW UPON MY LIFE.

Freedom

If the Son sets you free, you really will be free.
JOHN 8:36 HCSB

- -

Many things can keep us from being free. Certain relationships can be so unhealthy that they rob us of our freedom. Addiction—whether to alcohol or drugs or to a particular behavior—can also turn us into slaves. We may feel as though our work is a form of slavery, or physical illness can restrict our lives. Often our society promises us freedom. Buy this product, and your problems will go away. Eat this; don't eat that. Do this; don't do that. And yet somehow we never *feel* free. What's promised never materializes. But when Jesus promises to set us free, He keeps His promise. As we follow Him, He will lead us into new paths, paths that lead to true freedom. All we have to do is follow Him—and say thank You, over and over again.

JESUS, THANK YOU FOR SETTING ME FREE.

Knit Together in Love

That their hearts might be comforted, being knit together in love, and unto all riches of the full assurance of understanding, to the acknowledgement of the mystery of God, and of the Father, and of Christ.

COLOSSIANS 2:2 KJV

The comfort God gives us is another reason we have to feel gratitude. In this life, God will always be a mystery to us; we will never fully understand who He is. And that's a good thing, because God is too big for us to put Him into a box. As we acknowledge that truth, we gain new riches in understanding. We are knit together in love with others and with God. Then, even in the midst of trouble and confusion, our hearts will be comforted. We can thank God that even though there is so much we don't understand, we do understand that we are loved.

THANK YOU, GOD, FOR KNITTING
MY HEART CLOSE TO YOURS.

What Comes Next

We continue to shout our praise even when we're hemmed in with troubles, because we know how troubles can develop passionate patience in us, and how that patience in turn forges the tempered steel of virtue, keeping us alert for whatever God will do next. In alert expectancy such as this, we're never left feeling shortchanged. Quite the contrary—we can't round up enough containers to hold everything God generously pours into our lives through the Holy Spirit!

ROMANS 5:3–5 MSG

When we "shout our praise," we're thanking God at the top of our lungs for all He has done for us and all we know He *will* do for us. We usually think of gratitude as an emotion we feel about something in the past or present; but in this case, the Bible is telling us to feel grateful for things that haven't yet happened. In the midst of difficult times, we can be grateful for what we are learning, but we can also be thankful for whatever God will do next. That attitude of grateful expectancy, looking forward to God's actions in the future, brightens dark times and gives us hope.

REMIND ME, GOD, THAT YOU ARE ALWAYS WORKING. THANK YOU FOR WHATEVER YOU DO NEXT.

Heavenly Riches

*You know the grace of our Lord Jesus Christ, that
though He was rich, yet for your sake He became poor,
so that you through His poverty might become rich.*

2 CORINTHIANS 8:9 NASB

Jesus gives us so many reasons to be grateful. Think about what it meant for Him to become a human. First, He set aside all the riches and power of heaven. He could have been born into an important wealthy family; He could have chosen to have earthly wealth and prestige. Instead, He became a poor person, a common laborer, someone people barely noticed for the first thirty years of His life. He did this so that He could identify with ordinary people. He did this so you and I could share His heavenly riches.

THANK YOU, JESUS, FOR BECOMING
POOR SO THAT I COULD BE RICH.

The Here and Now

I have learned to be content whatever the circumstances.
PHILIPPIANS 4:11 NIV

Sometimes we're so focused on the future that we forget to notice what we have right now in the present moment. We act as though happiness is always somewhere up ahead, instead of finding it in the here and now. Having goals for the future can be healthy and productive, but at the same time we should learn to follow the apostle Paul's example and be content with the circumstances we've been given *now*. "Be grateful for what you already have while you pursue your goals," writes author Roy T. Bennett. "If you aren't grateful for what you already have, what makes you think you would be happy with more?"

TEACH ME, LORD, TO BE GRATEFUL
FOR THE HERE AND NOW.

Divine Generosity

It was all his doing; we had nothing to do with it. He gave us a good bath, and we came out of it new people, washed inside and out by the Holy Spirit. Our Savior Jesus poured out new life so generously. God's gift has restored our relationship with him and given us back our lives. And there's more life to come—an eternity of life!

TITUS 3:5–7 MSG

When our hearts are full of complaints and worries, when our lives feel small and restricted, it might be a good idea to spend some time meditating on this verse. Write it on a note card and tape it somewhere you'll see it often. Read and reread it. Pray over it. Absorb this reality: Jesus has made us clean through the Holy Spirit; we are new people, free to live new lives. God is close to us in a new way, and all the riches of life still lie ahead. Divine generosity is everywhere we turn.

LORD, REPLACE MY WORRY AND RESENTMENT WITH GRATITUDE FOR ALL THAT YOU HAVE DONE FOR ME.

The Words of Jesus

"The words I have spoken to you—
they are full of the Spirit and life."
JOHN 6:63 NIV

The words Jesus spoke to us in the Gospels can be another inspiration for our gratitude. How good it is that we have these records of the words He spoke when He was with us on earth! As we read and reread them, they sink into our hearts and minds. We gain access to the Spirit. We have a deeper understanding of life. We come alive in new and profound ways. We learn how to follow Jesus more closely. How grateful we should be that we have this glimpse into the mind and Spirit of Jesus! How good God is to have given us His Word where we can find the wisdom we need for life!

JESUS, THANK YOU FOR THE WORDS YOU
SPOKE WHILE YOU WALKED THIS EARTH WITH
PHYSICAL FEET. MAY I DAILY LEARN FROM YOU.

The Vine

"I am the Vine, you are the branches. When you're joined with me and I with you, the relation intimate and organic, the harvest is sure to be abundant. Separated, you can't produce a thing. Anyone who separates from me is deadwood, gathered up and thrown on the bonfire. But if you make yourselves at home with me and my words are at home in you, you can be sure that whatever you ask will be listened to and acted upon."

JOHN 15:5–7 MSG

- -

The Bible talks about our connection to Jesus as something living and organic, something even closer than the connections we share with family. In other places in the Bible, this relationship is referred to as the body of Christ, where each body part and organ is needed and necessary, all interdependent; but here Jesus uses the metaphor of the Vine, something living and green and growing. Each of us is an interdependent branch of that Vine, drawing our life from Jesus, making our home in Jesus. How thankful we can be for this amazing intimacy with Christ!

JESUS, MY HEART OVERFLOWS WITH GRATITUDE FOR THE LIVING RELATIONSHIP I HAVE WITH YOU.

Forgiveness and Gratitude

Then Peter came to Jesus and asked, "Lord, how many times shall I forgive my brother or sister who sins against me? Up to seven times?" Jesus answered, "I tell you, not seven times, but seventy-seven times."
MATTHEW 18:21–22 NIV

At first glance, you might not think gratitude has much to do with forgiveness. But as Oprah Winfrey once said, "True forgiveness is when you can say, 'Thank you for that experience.' " Where there is a thankful heart, there is no room for unforgiveness. Gratitude lets go of resentment and anger. It replaces "That wasn't fair, God!" with "Thank You, Lord, for the chance to learn more about myself, about You, about others." Gratitude is a willingness to see the good even in what irks us or hurts us. It releases our need to be right. It surrenders to the will of God in every circumstance.

TEACH ME, LORD, TO SAY THANK
YOU EVEN WHEN IT'S HARD.

Noisy Gratitude

Praise the LORD. Praise God in his sanctuary; praise him in his mighty heavens. Praise him for his acts of power; praise him for his surpassing greatness. Praise him with the sounding of the trumpet, praise him with the harp and lyre, praise him with timbrel and dancing, praise him with the strings and pipe, praise him with the clash of cymbals, praise him with resounding cymbals.

PSALM 150:1–5 NIV

Sometimes gratitude is a quiet sort of emotion, a peaceful, calm feeling that fills our hearts when we are alone. Other times, though, we may want to express our thankfulness loudly and publicly. This verse from Psalms talks about noisy gratitude, the kind of thankfulness that bursts into song, that clangs cymbals, that blows trumpets, that dances and bangs and makes a ruckus. No matter how we praise Him, God loves to hear our voices!

MAY I PRAISE YOU, LORD, BOTH QUIETLY
AND LOUDLY, EVERY CHANCE I GET.

New!

Therefore, if anyone is in Christ, he is a new creation; old things have passed away, and look, new things have come. Everything is from God, who reconciled us to Himself through Christ and gave us the ministry of reconciliation.

2 CORINTHIANS 5:17–18 HCSB

All of us have made mistakes. We may feel guilt for the times we have hurt others. We may also feel shame for things that have been done to us, things that made us feel small or soiled or broken. But in Christ, all those things are gone. We become brand-new people, ready for an all-new life in Christ. We are brought close to God and are given the work of helping others come close to God and to one another. The past no longer has the power to hurt us. Gratitude replaces shame and guilt.

THANK YOU, JESUS, FOR MAKING ME A NEW PERSON, FOR GIVING ME A NEW LIFE.

Beloved Children

So you have not received a spirit that makes you fearful slaves.
Instead, you received God's Spirit when he adopted you as his
own children. Now we call him, "Abba, Father." For his Spirit
joins with our spirit to affirm that we are God's children.

ROMANS 8:15–16 NLT

How thankful we can be that we are truly God's children! We may still refer to God as "Lord," as a term of respect, but God says that we are not servants or slaves; instead, we are His beloved children. We have the right to call God "Daddy"! The Holy Spirit within us joins with our own spirits, letting us know that we are loved, that we have an intimate relationship with the Creator of the universe. This is the reality we are called to experience as God's own children, our hearts overflowing with love, joy, and gratitude.

THANK YOU, FATHER, THAT YOU
HAVE MADE ME YOUR CHILD.

Gifts That Keep Giving

God's various gifts are handed out everywhere; but they all originate in God's Spirit. God's various ministries are carried out everywhere; but they all originate in God's Spirit. God's various expressions of power are in action everywhere; but God himself is behind it all. Each person is given something to do that shows who God is: Everyone gets in on it, everyone benefits. All kinds of things are handed out by the Spirit, and to all kinds of people! The variety is wonderful.

1 CORINTHIANS 12:4–7 MSG

Gifts are what inspire gratitude. They are given freely, never earned; they have no strings attached. And our God loves to give. He hands out gifts everywhere, and His gifts keep on giving, so that through God, we too become a part of the never-ending celebration of giving and gratitude. Just think about it! You have been given something that allows you to show others who God is. It's your own unique gift, given to you by God—and now you get to pass it on.

I AM SO GRATEFUL, GOD, FOR THE GIFTS
YOU HAVE GIVEN ME. MAY I USE YOUR GIFTS
TO SHOW YOUR LOVE TO OTHERS.

Our Body

No one ever hates his own flesh but provides and cares for it.

EPHESIANS 5:29 HCSB

- -

Are you grateful for your body? Despite what this scripture verse says, too many of us have in fact been taught to hate our own bodies. We hold them up against an impossible Barbie-doll standard, and when they fall short, we criticize them and feel shame. Our bodies, however, are amazing creations, capable of so many wonderful things. Think about it—and perhaps consider thanking God for your body's ability to move and for its amazing senses of sight, smell, hearing, touch, and taste. Be grateful for all the ways it serves you so faithfully. And express your gratitude by providing and caring for your body's needs.

THANK YOU, GOD, FOR THIS FLESH YOU CREATED.
MAY I HONOR IT AND CARE FOR IT RESPONSIBLY.

Wants and Needs

*God will supply all your needs according to
His riches in glory in Christ Jesus.*

PHILIPPIANS 4:19 NASB

Sometimes it's difficult to tell our wants from our needs. God never promises that we'll have everything that tickles our fancy—but the Bible does say that God will give us everything we truly need. We can count on Him to draw from His great eternal wealth on our behalf. The Greek word that's translated here as "glory" meant literally "brightness, splendor, the manifestation of God." Think about that! Through Jesus, we have direct access to the Light that is God. Life may still be challenging. But we can be grateful that God is giving us exactly what we need when we need it.

I AM SO GRATEFUL, JESUS, THAT I CAN SHARE
IN YOUR SPLENDOR AND LIGHT. THANK YOU
FOR GIVING ME EVERYTHING I NEED.

Don't Panic!

"I, your God, have a firm grip on you and I'm not letting go.
I'm telling you, 'Don't panic. I'm right here to help you.' "
ISAIAH 41:13 MSG

Life can be scary. Sometimes it seems as though we meet uncertainty and conflict everywhere we turn. It's easy to feel anxious, and some days we may find ourselves sinking into panic, asking ourselves if everything is going to turn out all right—or if we and the rest of the world are heading for disaster. When you feel like that, make a point to read verses like this one. Let them soak into your mind. God has a firm grip on you! He will not drop you. You don't need to panic. Instead, you can let gratitude replace your fear and anxiety. . .and allow yourself to rest in God's capable hands.

YOU KNOW, LORD, HOW FRIGHTENING THE
WORLD IS THESE DAYS. THANK YOU THAT YOU
ARE STILL IN CONTROL. HELP ME TO TRUST YOU.

When We Are Weak

Jotham strengthened himself because he did
not waver in obeying the LORD his God.

2 CHRONICLES 27:6 HCSB

- - - - - - - - - - - - - - - - - - -

Do you ever feel too spiritually and emotionally weak to be grateful? We all have times like that, but the Bible tells us a secret: we will strengthen ourselves by obeying God, no matter how weak we may feel on the inside. In the Gospels, Jesus told us what it means to obey God. He said that all the commandments can be summed up in two simple things: to love God with all our hearts and minds, and to love others as ourselves (Matthew 22:37–39). As we make those two things the focus of our lives, our weakness will turn to strength, and our heart will once more spill over with gratitude for God's blessings.

WHEN I AM WEAK, LORD, REMIND ME
TO FOLLOW YOU MORE CLOSELY.

Inconceivably Magnificent

"No eye has seen, no ear has heard, and no mind has imagined what God has prepared for those who love him."

1 CORINTHIANS 2:9 NLT

Despite all its problems, this world is a wonderful and beautiful place. But the Bible tells us that heaven will be incomparably more wonderful. We can't even imagine how lovely it will be. It's like trying to picture a color you've never seen or imagine a sense you don't have; we just can't come up with an image for something we've never seen or heard. Whatever we imagine will fall short of the reality we will one day discover. So when you feel grateful for this world's wondrous beauty, let your mind open to the unimaginable beauty of the next world—and thank God for all He has prepared for us there.

I CAN'T IMAGINE WHAT HEAVEN WILL BE LIKE, GOD, BUT I'M SO GLAD THAT ONE DAY I'LL FIND OUT!

Patience

Patient endurance is what you need now, so that you will continue to do God's will. Then you will receive all that he has promised.

HEBREWS 10:36 NLT

- -

Life isn't all a bed of roses—and following Jesus won't automatically make life easier. Instead, the Bible tells us to let the hard times build our ability to endure. We learn to keep going, confident that God knows what He's doing, and to keep our eyes fixed on Him rather than the difficulties around us. Gratitude can help us develop patience; even during the hard times, we can thank God for the way He is working behind the scenes, and we can anticipate what He is bringing into being for the future.

GOD, PLEASE TEACH ME PATIENCE AND ENDURANCE. HELP ME TO BECOME THE STRONG FOLLOWER YOU WANT ME TO BE. AND THANK YOU, FATHER, FOR ALL THAT YOU ARE DOING, ALL THE TIME.

Waiting on the Lord

They that wait upon the LORD shall renew their strength;
they shall mount up with wings as eagles; they shall run,
and not be weary; and they shall walk, and not faint.

ISAIAH 40:31 KJV

- - - - - - - - - - - - - - - - - - -

When life seems exhausting, how do we renew our strength? The Bible tells us there's a secret to this: we wait upon the Lord. The Hebrew word that is translated "wait" meant literally "to eagerly expect, to look eagerly, to wait patiently." That's what it takes to keep us going when life is overwhelming: a patient eagerness for God. Even when our lives seem dry and empty, we can continue to look eagerly for God's presence. Doing so will give us new strength. We can rejoice in our ability to keep walking, running, and even flying. We can thank God for giving us the strength we need to keep going.

WHEN I'M WEARY, LORD, REMIND ME TO WAIT
FOR YOU. GIVE ME AN EAGER EXPECTATION
AS I PLACE MY CONFIDENCE IN YOU.

First Things First

"Do not worry then, saying, 'What will we eat?' or 'What will we drink?' or 'What will we wear for clothing?' ... But seek first His kingdom and His righteousness, and all these things will be added to you."

MATTHEW 6:31, 33 NASB

It's easy to worry about material things. Maybe we have enough to eat and drink—but we still worry about the bills that are piling up. We wonder if we'll be able to afford things like braces and new clothes and college for our kids. As the external world grows more uncertain, we worry that we won't have enough to provide for our families. Jesus understood those concerns, and He told us, "Don't worry about those things! Instead, focus on My kingdom. When you do, I'll take care of the rest." How do we cultivate this attitude, though, when worries are everywhere we turn? Once again, the answer is gratitude. Instead of worrying, we can thank God that He is caring for our material needs.

> I AM SO GRATEFUL, JESUS, THAT YOU UNDERSTAND MY FINANCIAL CONCERNS. HELP ME TO GIVE THEM TO YOU SO I CAN BE FREE TO HELP YOU BUILD YOUR KINGDOM.

Nature

Let the heavens be glad, and let the earth rejoice; let the sea roar, and all it contains; let the field exult, and all that is in it. Then all the trees of the forest will sing for joy.

PSALM 96:11–12 NASB

- -

Our modern age often thinks of nature as being inanimate, without emotion or knowing, but the Bible describes nature as actively praising God with its very being. When gratitude seems difficult to drum up, going out into nature may help. There, beneath a blue sky or towering clouds, in fields of waving grass and wildflowers, amid the green silence of a forest, or on a beach roaring with the sound of the surf, we can join in the song of praise that rises up from all creation.

LORD, I PRAISE YOU FOR THE BEAUTIFUL WORLD YOU MADE. MAY I TAKE TIME TO BE IN IT AND LEARN FROM IT.

Work

*GOD will lavish you with good things. . .
and blessed the work you take in hand.*

DEUTERONOMY 28:11–12 MSG

- - - - - - - - - - - - - - - - - - -

Our work is another reason to be grateful to God. Whether it's the job that allows us to earn our living, a creative activity like sewing or painting or writing a poem, or the daily work of caring for a home and a family, God is there with us in every task we take on. With each one, we have the opportunity to serve and praise God with our actions, no matter how ordinary they may seem. Through our work, God blesses both us and others. Perhaps we should make a habit, then, of thanking God as we begin each workday or at the outset of each new project. Just as we ask a blessing on our food, we could get in the habit of "saying grace" for our work as well.

THANK YOU FOR MY WORK, LORD GOD.
MAY I DO IT TO YOUR GLORY.

Beyond Our Imagination

[God] is able to do above and beyond all that we ask
or think according to the power that works in us.
EPHESIANS 3:20 HCSB

God may not answer our prayers just the way we had hoped. But when we look back at our lives, we can see that He was doing something better all along. He's not a magic genie who will grant our wishes— but His plans for us are not limited by our imaginations. He will do so much more than we'd hoped or dreamed. We can be grateful that our thoughts put no boundaries on His actions. His power is unfathomable, and His creativity is boundless! Who knows what He will do next?

THANK YOU, BELOVED GOD, THAT YOU ARE
DOING AMAZING THINGS IN MY LIFE. I AM EAGERLY
WAITING TO SEE WHAT YOU WILL DO TODAY.

Amen

"Amen, blessing and glory and wisdom and
thanksgiving and honor and power and might,
be to our God forever and ever. Amen."
REVELATION 7:12 NASB

- -

When we say "Amen," we are saying, "Let it be so." We are affirming that God knows what He is doing and that His words are true and dependable. As a way of practicing gratitude, we might make a habit of saying "amen" at odd moments throughout the day—when the traffic light turns red as we are rushing to work, when we sit down to pay our bills, or when our spouse exasperates us. "Amen" may be the last thing we feel like saying in those circumstances, but in doing so, we let God know we are open to whatever He wants to do in our lives. We are letting go of our impatience, anxiety, and frustration, and we are saying, "Thank You for making this circumstance exactly the way it is."

TEACH ME, LORD, TO SAY "AMEN" TO EACH
THING YOU BRING INTO MY LIFE.

Peace

*You will keep in perfect peace all who trust in
you, all whose thoughts are fixed on you!*

ISAIAH 26:3 NLT

So many things can steal our peace. But it's not the actual circumstances that rob us of the peace of mind we crave. Instead, it's our reactions to those circumstances. Worry, frustration, anger, resentment, jealousy, boredom—all these things can push peace out of our hearts. The solution is to respond instead to each circumstance with a "Thank You, Lord," which will turn our thoughts to God. Responding this way also increases our trust, helping us to grow in faith even in the midst of difficult circumstances. When our thoughts are fixed on God, He will send His peace into our hearts.

MAY I KNOW YOUR PERFECT PEACE, LORD, NO
MATTER WHAT IS HAPPENING IN MY LIFE.

Rooted in Love

I pray that you, being rooted and established in love, may have power, together with all the Lord's holy people, to grasp how wide and long and high and deep is the love of Christ, and to know this love that surpasses knowledge—that you may be filled to the measure of all the fullness of God.

EPHESIANS 3:17–19 NIV

It's difficult enough to believe in someone we've never seen, let alone believe that someone loves us. Some days it may be easier to believe, while other days we may need to rely on the faith of other people to help us believe. Either way, as we make gratitude to God our way of life, our roots continually grow deeper into love. We will never be able to fully understand it or grasp it—but we can nevertheless experience it. We can become filled up with the fullness of God. Isn't that amazing?

FILL ME WITH YOU, GOD. I WANT MY ROOTS
TO SINK DEEP INTO YOUR LOVE.

Light in the Dark

We couldn't be more sure of what we saw and heard—God's glory, God's voice. The prophetic Word was confirmed to us. You'll do well to keep focusing on it. It's the one light you have in a dark time as you wait for daybreak and the rising of the Morning Star in your hearts. The main thing to keep in mind here is that no prophecy of Scripture is a matter of private opinion. And why? Because it's not something concocted in the human heart. Prophecy resulted when the Holy Spirit prompted men and women to speak God's Word.

2 PETER 1:19–21 MSG

Do you ever wonder if the people who wrote the Bible really knew what they were talking about? Doubt is a normal thing, even a healthy thing—but in these verses the apostle Peter is telling us that we can believe the Bible's account of Jesus and His love. During those times when we may not be able to *feel* God, we can cling to verses like these. While we wait to see Jesus face-to-face, we can thank Him that we have His words of life and love as recorded in the Bible.

THANK YOU, JESUS, FOR YOUR WORD.
TEACH ME TO FOCUS ON IT SO THAT IT
LIGHTS UP EVEN MY DARK TIMES.

A Thanksgiving Chorus

Oh give thanks to the Lord, for He is good,
for His lovingkindness is everlasting.

PSALM 107:1 NASB

The theme of Psalm 107 is expressed in this first verse. The verses that follow give four reasons to give God thanks. Each instance begins with a cry of distress over the situation in which the people found themselves, followed by a summary of how God heard and answered prayer. At the end of each, the "thanksgiving chorus" that begins the psalm is repeated once again. We too can experience this pattern in our own lives, crying out for God's help and then singing our thanksgiving chorus when we see His deliverance.

YOU ARE SO GOOD, LORD. YOUR LOVE
AND KINDNESS NEVER END.

Our Children

*"I will pour out my Spirit on your descendants,
and my blessing on your children."*

ISAIAH 44:3 NLT

- - - - - - - - - - - - - - - - - -

It's easy to feel anxious about the children in our lives. After all, the world is full of dangers over which we have no control. The older our children grow, the less control we have. We worry about the decisions they may make; we wonder if they are safe and happy and healthy. But God has promised to bless our children. We can put them in His hands, thanking Him for His faithfulness and care. Just as He has blessed us and led us, so He also will lead our children. We can trust Him to pour out His Spirit on them.

THANK YOU FOR THE CHILDREN IN MY
LIFE, LORD, AND THANK YOU FOR LOVING
THEM EVEN MORE THAN I DO.

Counting Our Blessings

Fix your thoughts on what is true, and honorable, and right, and pure, and lovely, and admirable. Think about things that are excellent and worthy of praise.

PHILIPPIANS 4:8 NLT

It's difficult to feel grateful when we're preoccupied with our worries and complaints—but much easier when we focus on things that are true, honorable, right, pure, lovely, admirable, excellent, and worthy of praise. An old hymn puts it this way:

When upon life's billows you are tempest tossed,
When you are discouraged, thinking all is lost,
Count your many blessings, name them one by one,
And it will surprise you what the Lord hath done.
(Johnson Oatman Jr., 1897)

Some people have suggested that counting blessings is far more effective at night than counting sheep!

YOU HAVE BLESSED ME IN SO MANY WAYS, LORD. REMIND ME TO COUNT BLESSINGS RATHER THAN WORRIES OR COMPLAINTS.

Breath of Life

Yahweh my Lord is my strength; He makes my feet like those of a deer and enables me to walk on mountain heights!

HABAKKUK 3:19 HCSB

- -

The name God called Himself—Yahweh—means literally the "Living One," the "Life Giver." According to author Richard Rohr in his book *The Naked Now*, "Yahweh" was intended to be the sound of our breath: inhalation (Yah), exhalation (weh).* If this is true, then we spoke the name of God with our first breath, and it will be the last thing we speak when we die. God is the breath of our life, knit into the very fabric of our being. He is our strength, our life—and He makes us walk like a deer on mountain heights!

---

* Richard Rohr, *The Naked Now: Learning to See as the Mystics See* (Chestnut Ridge, NY: Crossroad, 2009).

> THANK YOU, BREATH OF LIFE, FOR FILLING ME WITH YOUR SPIRIT, FOR GIVING ME STRENGTH, FOR LIFTING ME UP.

Gratitude Bookends

They are to stand every morning to thank and to praise the Lord, and likewise at evening.

1 Chronicles 23:30 NASB

- -

Here's a good practice for us all: begin each day by saying thank You to the Lord, and end each day by doing the same. That way, our days are bookended by gratitude. It's a great way to start the day, one that will bring hope and energy to our mornings; and it's also a wonderful way to end the day, refocusing our minds on positive things so that we can settle down peacefully to sleep. Try it for the next week. As soon as you wake up, say something as short and simple as "Thank You, Lord," and then when you get into bed, repeat the same words. See if it changes the way you feel about life.

LORD, MAY EACH OF MY DAYS BEGIN
AND END WITH THANKSGIVING.

Wordless

Unless the LORD had been my help,
my soul had almost dwelt in silence.
PSALM 94:17 KJV

Sometimes life's situations stun us into silence. We're too overwhelmed to say thank You to God. We can't even manage to cry out for help. And yet even then, the Bible says that God will help us. He won't leave us in silence. His Spirit's quiet urging will pull our hearts to Him. The Spirit will even pray on our behalf with "groanings that cannot be expressed in words" (Romans 8:26 NLT). Eventually, He will give us the strength we need to put words to our situation. Once again we will be able to voice our gratitude to God.

THANK YOU, LORD OF LOVE, THAT YOU
DO NOT LEAVE MY SOUL IN SILENCE.

Prince of Peace

The peace of God, which transcends all understanding,
will guard your hearts and your minds in Christ Jesus.

PHILIPPIANS 4:7 NIV

- -

When we focus on things we can't do anything about, we end up feeling frustrated and worried. We lose our sense of peace. When we fret about things beyond our control, stress and tension can make us not only upset and anxious but even physically ill. Worry seems to come naturally enough, but let it be a cue that reminds us to turn our thoughts immediately to gratitude. In other words, each time we sense ourselves beginning to struggle with anxiety or frustration, we can quickly shift our focus to gratitude instead. As we make a habit of shifting our focus, God's peace, which goes beyond human understanding, will guard our thoughts.

THANK YOU, PRINCE OF PEACE, FOR
YOUR CONSTANT CARE. REMIND ME TO
TURN TO THANKSGIVING WHENEVER
ANXIETY OVERTAKES ME.

Light

*Ye are the light of the world. A city that
is set on an hill cannot be hid.*

MATTHEW 5:14 KJV

A lot of people have negative ideas about what Christians are like. Unfortunately, they often got those ideas from observing how Christians behave. Christians who are hypocritical in their actions and beliefs confuse people. Christians who are gloomy, angry, or judgmental can cause others to think that's what it means to follow Christ. But the Bible asks us to be light for the world. In today's tense and polarized world, being the light that we're called to be is even more important. May others see us shining with gratitude, joy, and love!

MAKE ME SHINE FOR YOU, LORD.

Open Up!

"It was I, the LORD your God, who rescued you. . . . Open your mouth wide, and I will fill it with good things."

PSALM 81:10 NLT

Sometimes we put limits on God. We don't believe He can change our situations. We doubt He can heal our wounds or break our bad habits. We think our circumstances are hopeless. But God asks us to remember all the ways He has rescued us in the past. And then He says, "Open your mouth wide! Stop nibbling at My grace when I have an abundance I'm waiting to give you. Don't put limits on Me. I want to fill your life with good things. Just wait and see all the ways I'm going to bless you. So open up!"

THANK YOU, LORD, THAT NOTHING
IS HOPELESS TO YOU. HELP ME TO BE
OPEN TO YOUR AMAZING GRACE.

Old Age

I was young and now I am old, yet I have never seen the righteous forsaken or their children begging bread.

PSALM 37:25 NIV

Do you ever worry about your old age? Are you afraid of the ways your body may fail you? Do you fret about how your children will manage when you are too old to be there for them, when you may have to rely on them instead of the other way around? In this verse, the psalmist asks us to pay attention to his witness. He knows from experience: God does not abandon anyone in their old age, nor will He leave their children without the help they need. God will never ever forsake either our children or us. We can trust the future to Him—and thank Him for the lifetime of blessings He has planned for us.

THANK YOU, LOVING GOD, THAT YOU WILL BE WITH ME WHEN I AM OLD. THANK YOU THAT YOU WILL NEVER FORSAKE ME OR THE PEOPLE I LOVE.

Spirit Work

*It is God who is working in you, enabling you both
to desire and to work out His good purpose.*

PHILIPPIANS 2:13 HCSB

- -

Sometimes we get the idea that God expects us to pull ourselves up by our own bootstraps. We act as though it's all up to us—and when we fail, as we always do sooner or later, then we're filled with guilt. God wants us to stop trying so hard and relax into Him. God is the one who does the work, not us. God's Spirit is the one who even makes us *want* to do His will, and He's the one who will continue to work in our lives and in our hearts, shaping us into the people we were created to be. As we rely more and more on Him, as we turn to Him daily in gratitude, He will do amazing things in our lives.

LORD, SHAPE ME INTO THE PERSON YOU
WANT ME TO BE. TEACH ME TO SURRENDER
TO YOUR SPIRIT AT WORK IN MY LIFE.

Crossroads

I've brought you today to the crossroads of Blessing and Curse.
DEUTERONOMY 11:26 MSG

Sooner or later, we all stand at this crossroads. Will we go the way of God's blessing—or will we stubbornly choose our own way. . .and suffer the consequences? God never wants to curse us. He never wishes that painful or destructive things would enter our lives. Always, always, He yearns to bless us. But sometimes our own actions lead to unavoidably negative results. Even then, though, God does not abandon us. The Bible tells the story of God's people getting off track over and over, and over and over again He draws them back to Himself and gets them back on course. He'll do the same for us.

OH LORD, THANK YOU THAT WHEN I MAKE WRONG CHOICES, EVEN THEN YOU DO NOT ABANDON ME.

Hope

I pray that God, the source of hope, will fill you completely with joy and peace because you trust in him. Then you will overflow with confident hope through the power of the Holy Spirit.
ROMANS 15:13 NLT

- -

This word, *hope*, means "the expectation of something good." Notice in this verse that hope is not something we're supposed to work up in ourselves; instead, it *comes from God*. He is the one who gives us the confidence to believe we can trust Him. His Spirit in us gives us power to overflow with hope! Living hope-filled lives means we're constantly expecting God to bless us—and He will. He will give us more and more reasons to be grateful, for hope and gratitude go hand in hand. We expect something good—and we're grateful for it, even ahead of time.

I AM SO GRATEFUL, SPIRIT OF GOD, FOR
THE POWER YOU GIVE ME TO HOPE.

Flourishing

"I will be like the dew to Israel; he will blossom like a lily. Like a cedar of Lebanon he will send down his roots; his young shoots will grow. His splendor will be like an olive tree, his fragrance like a cedar of Lebanon. People will dwell again in his shade; they will flourish like the grain, they will blossom like the vine."

HOSEA 14:5–7 NIV

These are lovely verses, filled with reasons to feel gratitude to God. In this passage of scripture, God promises to refresh us and make us blossom. He vows that we will grow both roots and branches, our lives spreading deeper and wider so that we have the ability to bless others. He tells us that blessing always spreads outward: not only will we blossom, but we will also help others to blossom. Our lives will have meaning. We will be fruitful and creative, contributing to the kingdom of heaven here on earth.

LORD OF LOVE, THANK YOU FOR ALL THE MANY WAYS YOU BLESS ME. MY HEART OVERFLOWS WITH GRATITUDE.

Gratitude Feasts

Feast there in the Presence of God, your God.
Celebrate everything that you and your families have
accomplished under the blessing of God, your God.
Deuteronomy 12:7 MSG

Sometimes we need to take time for special moments of gratitude, celebrations of all God has done for us and for our families and of all we have accomplished. Maybe we do this on Thanksgiving or at Christmas—but it might also be good to have more informal celebrations, our own intimate gatherings of gratitude. Maybe we'll invite friends and extended family, or maybe it will be just our immediate families, sharing a special meal. Maybe we want to go for a walk by ourselves or spend time alone, remembering all the blessings God has given us. However we choose to celebrate, these "gratitude feasts" can be times of remembrance that strengthen our hearts for the days ahead.

YOU HAVE BLESSED US IN SO MANY
WAYS, CREATOR GOD, AND YOU HAVE
HELPED US ACCOMPLISH SO MUCH!

Playful Spirits

"But for you who revere my name, the sun of
righteousness will rise with healing in its rays.
And you will go out and frolic like well-fed calves."
MALACHI 4:2 NIV

Some days, it may seem as though we carry the weight of the world upon our shoulders. We plod along, our steps heavy, our hearts even heavier. But God doesn't want us to linger in these dreary times. Instead, He wants to shine His light on us. He yearns to heal us and lift our heavy loads; He wants to nourish our spirits and bodies, making them both healthy. And not only does He long to make us happy, but He also wants to give us spirits so joyful that we feel like playing like children again. And He will do all these things as we turn to Him, revering His name.

GOD, WHEN I'M DOWNHEARTED, REMIND ME THAT YOU ARE ALREADY PLANNING WAYS TO BLESS ME YET AGAIN, SO THAT ONE DAY SOON, I'LL FEEL LIKE PLAYING.

A Blossoming Spirit

A cheerful heart is good medicine, but a
broken spirit saps a person's strength.
PROVERBS 17:22 NLT

- - - - - - - - - - - - - - - - - - -

Some of us seem to be born with naturally optimistic and cheery natures, while others of us struggle with pessimism and negativity. If you're one of the "Eeyore" sorts of people, always sighing and seeing the dark side of life, there are ways you can counteract this tendency. You can form new thought habits, focusing on all there is to be grateful for in life. You might want to make a list of things you're thankful for and refer to it often. Or you could keep a gratitude journal, daily jotting down everything good, even the littlest things, that happened that day. Make a habit of telling God thank You often—and you may find that your cheerful spirit will begin to blossom.

GIVE ME A CHEERFUL SPIRIT, LORD.
MAKE ME STRONG IN YOUR JOY.

The Natural World

"The wild animals honor me, the jackals and the owls, because I provide water in the wilderness and streams in the wasteland."

ISAIAH 43:20 NIV

- -

Take a moment to think about the wild animals that live around you (even if they're just pigeons and squirrels). We are often unaware of these busy lives going on around us, worms munching through the soil, birds eating worms, and squirrels burying nuts in the earth—and foxes and hawks consuming birds and squirrels. The Bible says that all these creatures honor God with their lives—and in return, He provides for them. Our world is made so intricately, with each aspect of nature interdependent with all the rest, and we too are a part of that interwoven web. May we appreciate nature as the gift from God that it truly is, and may we honor God's world as it honors Him!

THANK YOU, CREATOR, FOR THE NATURAL WORLD AROUND ME. TEACH ME TO SEE IT WITH FRESH EYES, AND SHOW ME WAYS TO CARE FOR IT RESPONSIBLY.

Desert Times

*"I will open up rivers for them on the high plateaus.
I will give them fountains of water in the valleys. I
will fill the desert with pools of water. Rivers fed by
springs will flow across the parched ground."*

ISAIAH 41:18 NLT

We all have times in our lives that seem dry and barren. We look around and have trouble seeing many reasons to feel grateful. Maybe our life's circumstances are hard and challenging, or maybe nothing is really wrong and yet our emotions seem to have dried up inside us, leaving everything looking a little flat and bleak. Whatever the case, we can cling to promises like the one found in this verse. God will not leave us forever in these desert times. Soon He will refresh us with pools of grace and rivers of His mercy. We just have to be patient.

TEACH ME, FATHER, TO WAIT FOR YOUR
GRACE AND MERCY WATERING MY LIFE. I
THANK YOU FOR ALL YOU ARE DOING, EVEN
IN THE DRY, BARREN TIMES OF MY LIFE.

Giving

Give freely and spontaneously. Don't have a stingy heart. The way you handle matters like this triggers GOD, your God's, blessing in everything you do, all your work and ventures. There are always going to be poor and needy people among you. So I command you: Always be generous, open purse and hands, give to your neighbors in trouble, your poor and hurting neighbors.

DEUTERONOMY 15:10–11 MSG

We've seen that gratitude works well with other qualities. Another quality that could almost be seen as the flip side of gratitude is generosity. We have been given so much—and now God asks us to turn it around and give as freely as we have received. Our generous God wants us to pass along His blessings to others; He wants us to reflect His self-giving love to everyone we meet. This is the best way we can express our gratitude for all we have been given.

GENEROUS GOD, GIVE ME OPPORTUNITIES TODAY TO GIVE TO OTHERS. YOU HAVE GIVEN ME SO MUCH—MAY I BE EQUALLY AS GENEROUS IN ALL MY INTERACTIONS WITH EVERYONE I ENCOUNTER.

Fresh and Green

The righteous will flourish like a palm tree, they will grow like a cedar of Lebanon; planted in the house of the LORD, they will flourish in the courts of our God. They will still bear fruit in old age, they will stay fresh and green.

PSALM 92:12–14 NIV

Our God never stops blessing us. From the moment we entered this world, He has been with us, always close by even when we did not realize that His presence was with us. As we look back, our hearts are filled with gratitude—and we can look forward with the same sense of thankfulness, for God will continue to bless us through all the days of our lives. This verse promises that even in old age, we will bear "fruit"; we will remain "fresh and green," despite the years. We will not just survive; we will flourish!

THANK YOU, GOD OF LOVE, THAT YOU HAVE BEEN WITH ME THROUGHOUT MY LIFE. THANK YOU THAT I CAN ANTICIPATE THE YEARS AHEAD, EVEN AS I HEAD INTO OLD AGE, WITH GRATEFUL EAGERNESS FOR THE NEW WAYS YOU WILL BLESS ME.

Ups and Downs

Is anyone among you suffering? Then he must pray.
Is anyone cheerful? He is to sing praises.
JAMES 5:13 NASB

No matter what we are experiencing, we can use it as a trigger that points our focus toward God. Are you having a "blue" day when nothing looks right and everything seems wrong? Then take it to God in prayer. Tell Him about your feelings. Or are you having one of those days when the whole world seems to smile and you find yourself humming as you go about your work? Take that to God as well; lift your heart up to Him in praise and gratitude. Each emotion you feel can act as a tether that tugs your heart closer to the Lord. As you make a habit of telling God what you're feeling, you may find that your emotions no longer sway your heart to and fro. Instead, you'll have an inner steadiness that relies on God no matter what your emotions may be.

THANK YOU FOR THE GIFT OF MY
EMOTIONS, GOD. MAY I REMEMBER TO
GIVE EACH ONE OF THEM TO YOU.

When We're Depressed

God, who comforts the depressed,
comforted us by the coming of Titus.
2 CORINTHIANS 7:6 NASB

Many times, God uses other people to bless us and lift us up when we're feeling down. Even the apostle Paul experienced this. He was encouraged and strengthened when his good friend Titus joined him. God will do the same for us when we are downhearted. Good friends who care and listen to our troubles can lift our hearts with their understanding. Sometimes even a smile from a stranger at just the right moment can make all the difference. All we have to do is open our hearts to the individuals God brings into our lives—and then remember to thank God for blessing us through other people.

LORD, WHEN I AM FEELING SAD AND DREARY, PLEASE SEND ALONG SOMEONE WHO UNDERSTANDS, SOMEONE WHO CAN HELP.

Prayer

*The effective prayer of a righteous man can accomplish much.
Elijah was a man with a nature like ours, and he prayed
earnestly that it would not rain, and it did not rain on the
earth for three years and six months. Then he prayed again,
and the sky poured rain and the earth produced its fruit.*

JAMES 5:16–18 NASB

Prayer is a powerful tool that God has given us. It's not like rubbing a genie's magic bottle, though; we're not guaranteed to get exactly what we pray for. Through prayer, however, we join our hearts with God's. As we pray with the Spirit's leading, we lend our energies to the great, eternal song that is constantly going on in heaven, a prayer of blessing, praise, and gratitude that works to bring good even out of terrible situations. What an amazing privilege and honor God has given us!

THANK YOU, LORD, FOR ALLOWING ME TO
PARTICIPATE IN YOUR KINGDOM THROUGH
THE POWER OF PRAYER. I AM SO GRATEFUL
FOR THIS PRIVILEGE! TEACH ME TO PRAY
WISELY, IN LINE WITH YOUR SPIRIT.

Celebrating God

*GOD, your God, has been blessing you in your harvest and
in all your work, so make a day of it—really celebrate!*
DEUTERONOMY 16:15 MSG

Sometimes we need to set aside time to truly celebrate all that God
has done. We look at our work, and we realize how God has blessed
it. We see how He has been working in our families. We know that
we have been growing spiritually, and we are glad for God's leading.
There will inevitably be hard times again, times full of pain and
doubt and sorrow. But while the good times are here, we need to
express our praise and gratitude to God. Doing so will strengthen
us for whatever lies ahead.

I AM SO GRATEFUL, GOD, FOR ALL YOU HAVE BEEN
DOING IN MY LIFE. I WANT TO CELEBRATE YOU!

Manna

*"After all, our ancestors ate manna while they
journeyed through the wilderness! The Scriptures
say, 'Moses gave them bread from heaven to eat.'"*
JOHN 6:31 NLT

- -

The Bible's stories can give us hope and strength for our own lives. Although we're unlikely to be wandering hungry and thirsty in a literal desert, we do have times when we wonder how we're going to manage to get through the challenges of life. Perhaps we wonder where the money will come from to pay this month's bills—or maybe we doubt we have the emotional strength to keep going in a difficult situation. When times like these come, we can look at how God miraculously provided for His people in the wilderness. With joy and gratitude, we can claim that story as our own and wait to see how God will rescue us.

I NEED SOME "MANNA," LORD. I'VE BEEN
WANDERING IN THIS DESERT, AND I'M HUNGRY
AND DESPERATE. I NEED YOUR HELP.

Always Present

"It was I who taught Ephraim to walk, taking them by the arms; but they did not realize it was I who healed them."

HOSEA 11:3 NIV

Sometimes we have reasons to be grateful to God that we never realize. We often fail to appreciate all the ways He has been working behind the scenes to bring about His will in our lives. From the moment we took our first toddling steps when we were babies, He was there beside us. As we learned our first words, He was there. When we went to kindergarten, He rode the bus beside us. When we learned to drive, when we left home for the first time, and through all the days of our lives, He has been there, leading and guiding even when we were completely unaware of His presence.

LORD, I AM GRATEFUL FOR YOUR QUIET, HELPING PRESENCE IN MY LIFE.

An Intimate Relationship

"Oh, that we might know the LORD! Let us press on to know him. He will respond to us as surely as the arrival of dawn or the coming of rains in early spring."

HOSEA 6:3 NLT

We have the privilege of being in an intimate relationship with the Creator of the universe. That's an amazing fact! The more we yearn to know Him, the more He reaches out to us. The more we struggle to grow closer to Him, the more He helps us to do just that. Even when our hearts grow cold or full of doubt, He continues to work to bring us to Him. We can be so grateful that He longs for us even more than we long for Him. He is working moment by moment to draw us close to Him—and His love is as reliable as the sunrise, as dependable as spring rainfall.

CREATOR GOD, THANK YOU THAT YOU LOVE ME AND WANT TO BE MY FRIEND.

The Gratitude Song

Let everything that has breath praise the Lord.

PSALM 150:6 NIV

- -

Take time to step outside sometime today. Listen to the wind in the trees, to the sound of birds; look for signs of insect life and watch for small, furry creatures going about their lives. Hear traffic going by and people calling. Now imagine that all these sights and sounds blend together into a chorus to God. This Bible verse calls on the entire living planet to lift up a song of praise and gratitude to the Lord. Everything that participates in respiration—plants and all manner of creatures, as well as human beings—is asked to take part in this song. Carry this song with you today.

GREAT LORD OF LOVE, MAY I SING
OUT MY GRATITUDE TO YOU.

Generosity and Blessing

No one is to show up in the Presence of GOD empty-handed; each man must bring as much as he can manage, giving generously in response to the blessings of GOD.

DEUTERONOMY 16:17 MSG

Again and again, the Bible tells us how we are to respond to God's blessings: we express our gratitude by giving generously back to God by giving to others. We never need to show up in God's presence empty handed, because He always gives us plenty to pass along to others. We'll never be able to match His generosity, but we can allow ourselves to become free-flowing conduits of blessing, a bright river of generosity that streams from God through us and out to others around us. Our God has been so good to us—and we express our gratitude by passing along His goodness.

GENEROUS LORD, MAKE US MORE LIKE YOU,
CONSTANTLY GIVING TO EVERYONE WE MEET.

Rewards

"There truly is a reward for those who live for God."
PSALM 58:11 NLT

- -

No one can work endlessly without seeing any rewards. If we try, we get tired and burned out. That's why it's a good idea to stop now and then and notice the rewards of our labor. Maybe those rewards aren't exactly what we'd hoped for. Maybe we haven't earned as much money as we'd wished, maybe no one has noticed and praised us for our efforts the way we'd dreamed, and maybe the results we'd hoped for still haven't been realized. But if we look, we'll see that God has rewarded us in some way. As we take time to be grateful, we'll be encouraged to continue working.

THANK YOU, GOD, FOR REWARDING MY EFFORTS.
HELP ME TO KEEP WORKING FOR YOU.

Praise Song

Praise the LORD from the heavens; praise him in the heights above. Praise him, all his angels; praise him, all his heavenly hosts. Praise him, sun and moon; praise him, all you shining stars. Praise him, you highest heavens and you waters above the skies. Let them praise the name of the LORD, for at his command they were created. . . . Praise the LORD from the earth, you great sea creatures and all ocean depths, lightning and hail, snow and clouds, stormy winds that do his bidding, you mountains and all hills, fruit trees and all cedars, wild animals and all cattle, small creatures and flying birds, kings of the earth and all nations, you princes and all rulers on earth, young men and women, old men and children. Let them praise the name of the LORD.

PSALM 148:1–5, 7–13 NIV

Take a moment to sing this great song of praise and gratitude in your heart. Let it fill your thoughts. Continue to dwell on it throughout the day.

> TEACH ME TO DAILY SING YOUR
> SONG OF PRAISE, LORD.

Humble Work

*"God blesses those who are humble,
for they will inherit the whole earth."*
MATTHEW 5:5 NLT

- -

Do you ever feel as though you spend your life doing laundry, cleaning up the kitchen, and vacuuming floors? These humble tasks that need to be done again and again and again can grow tedious. And yet even here, our God meets us. In the quiet, repetitive work of caring for a household, He blesses us, and we can be grateful for these ordinary chores. They are expressions of love to our family, and they mirror God's constant loving care that He bestows on each one of us. All work, no matter how humble, can be a source of blessing.

THANK YOU, GOD, FOR MY HOME AND
FAMILY. MAY THE WORK I DO TO CARE
FOR THEM REFLECT YOUR LOVE.

Reminders

Let all that I am praise the LORD; with my whole heart, I will praise his holy name. Let all that I am praise the LORD; may I never forget the good things he does for me. He forgives all my sins and heals all my diseases. He redeems me from death and crowns me with love and tender mercies. He fills my life with good things. My youth is renewed like the eagle's!

PSALM 103:1–5 NLT

- -

Verses like these are good ones to memorize. Write them on note cards and tape them to your walls or the visor of your car. Copy them in your journal. Repeat them to yourself as you go about your day, or as you lie awake at night, waiting for sleep to claim you. Let them sink deep into your being, for these verses are a wonderful reminder of all God has done for us. He has forgiven us, healed us, redeemed us, crowned us, filled our lives with good things, and renewed us. We have so many reasons to be grateful!

LORD, THANK YOU FOR YOUR CONSTANT
GENEROUS GRACE. I AM SO GRATEFUL
FOR ALL YOU HAVE DONE FOR ME.

Curses into Blessings

GOD, your God, refused to listen to Balaam but turned the curse into a blessing—how GOD, your God, loves you!
DEUTERONOMY 23:5 MSG

Sometimes we encounter people in life who wish us ill. They may actually curse us, or they may simply express their anger and resentment in ways that make us *feel* cursed. No one likes to find themselves in situations like these, and when we do, it's easy to become defensive. We don't have to return anger for anger, though, for God promises that even now, we can be grateful for His ongoing blessing. Despite the words or emotions of others, He will turn things around and bring blessing out of curses. No human negativity can limit His grace and power.

GOD, WHEN I'M TEMPTED TO GET DEFENSIVE, REMIND ME THAT I DON'T NEED TO, FOR YOU TURN CURSES INTO BLESSINGS.

The End of Our Rope

"You're blessed when you're at the end of your rope.
With less of you there is more of God and his rule."
MATTHEW 5:3 MSG

The Bible is full of paradoxes like the one expressed in this verse. We're blessed when we're at the end of our rope? How can that be? When we've run out of resources, when our last nerve is gone— that's when God blesses us? Yes, He does. And when we find ourselves in those circumstances, we can actually be grateful. When we have used up everything we have, then we are forced to rely more fully on God. We can get out of His way so that He has free rein to work in us and through us to accomplish His will.

LORD, WHEN I'M AT THE END OF MY ROPE, REMIND ME THAT I CAN STILL PRAISE YOU. THANK YOU THAT YOU WILL ALWAYS PICK UP WHERE I LEAVE OFF.

Most Dear

"You're blessed when you feel you've lost what is most dear to you. Only then can you be embraced by the One most dear to you."

MATTHEW 5:4 MSG

Here's another paradox. How can we possibly be blessed when we've lost what is most dear to us? And yet Jesus tells us that's the case. As long as we're relying on other people for love and approval, we'll never really come to know the full measure of God's love and affirmation. Or maybe what's most dear to us is our job. . .or our home. . .or a role, such as being a mother or a grandmother. To lose one of those things would feel like a little death. And yet God promises that should that happen, He will be there. He will show us how dear we are to Him as He embraces us with His loving arms.

WHEN I LOSE WHAT I VALUE MOST, LORD, TEACH ME TO TURN TO YOU. THANK YOU THAT YOUR LOVE WILL NEVER FAIL.

Just as We Are

*"You're blessed when you're content with just who you are—
no more, no less. That's the moment you find yourselves
proud owners of everything that can't be bought."*

MATTHEW 5:5 MSG

- -

Are you content with who you are? Or do you find yourself wishing you were richer, smarter, thinner, more popular, more fashionable, more something? Most of us have times like that, but in this verse Jesus is calling us to be content with ourselves exactly as we are right now. We don't have to wait to lose ten pounds or to get a promotion at work or to buy a new wardrobe. In God's eyes, we are absolutely fine just as we are. As we learn to accept God's perspective on us, we come to realize how much we really have. Instead of focusing on what we don't have, we overflow with gratitude for all He has given us.

THANK YOU, LORD, THAT YOU LOVE ME AND
APPROVE OF ME JUST AS I AM. MAY I LEARN
TO SEE MYSELF THROUGH YOUR EYES.

Cooperation

*"You're blessed when you can show people how to cooperate
instead of compete or fight. That's when you discover
who you really are, and your place in God's family."*

MATTHEW 5:9 MSG

In today's world, we have plenty of opportunities to show others how to cooperate instead of argue and compete! Pick almost anything that's in the news, and you'll find that people have fierce and divided viewpoints on it. It's easy to be caught up in who's right (we are, of course!) and who's wrong (they are!)—but that perspective just leads to more arguments, tension, and polarization. Instead, God wants us to discover that we belong to something far greater than any divided perspective on any issue. We are a member of God's family, and our job is to spread unity and understanding.

HELP ME, JESUS, TO BECOME A BRIDGE
BETWEEN POINTS OF VIEW. MAY I BE A
CALMING INFLUENCE THAT POINTS OTHERS
AWAY FROM THEIR ARGUMENTS AND HELPS
THEM TO FOCUS INSTEAD ON YOU.

Spreading Blessing

*All these blessings will come down on you
and spread out beyond you because you have
responded to the Voice of GOD, your God.*

DEUTERONOMY 28:2 MSG

The Bible is full of the voice of God. We may also hear His voice in nature. We may hear Him speaking to our own hearts in a still, small voice. Or He may speak to us through other people or through the books we read. However we hear God talking to us, we are always called to respond. God wants to have a two-way conversation with us, a relationship that grows ever closer. When we do respond—with love, with obedience, with gratitude—we are blessed. And when we are blessed, we have blessings to share with others. Blessings always spread!

THANK YOU, LORD, FOR SPEAKING TO ME.
TEACH ME TO HEAR YOUR VOICE MORE
CLEARLY SO THAT I MAY RESPOND TO YOU.

The Perfect Friend

Lᴏʀᴅ, you are my God; I will exalt you and praise your name, for in perfect faithfulness you have done wonderful things, things planned long ago.

Iꜱᴀɪᴀʜ 25:1 ɴɪᴠ

Even our most faithful friends let us down sometimes. They're only human, after all, and sooner or later humans mess up, no matter how much they try not to. We can forgive our friends for being human (especially since we too are far from perfect!), but we can also be grateful that we have a friend who is perfectly faithful, who will never ever let us down, and who does wonderful things for us. Think about it: you have always been a part of God's plan. He has work prepared just for you, that only you can do, and He has plans to bless you in ways that only you can receive.

LORD MY GOD, I'M SO GRATEFUL THAT YOU ARE MY PERFECT FRIEND WHO NEVER FAILS ME. THANK YOU FOR ALL YOU HAVE PLANNED FOR MY LIFE.

Filled with the Spirit

Be filled with the Spirit, speaking to one another in psalms and hymns and spiritual songs, singing and making melody with your heart to the Lord; always giving thanks for all things in the name of our Lord Jesus Christ to God, even the Father.

EPHESIANS 5:18–20 NASB

- -

Notice how Paul words this portion of his letter to the church at Ephesus: "Be filled with the Spirit." It's a command—something that's up to us. For the Spirit is always there, always willing; we just have to make room for Him. Paul is telling us how to do this: by talking publicly about our gratitude for all God has done, encouraging one another with scripture and spiritual songs, while privately singing a song of thanksgiving in our deepest hearts. It's not complicated or hard to do. As we *always give thanks for all things*, the Spirit fills us.

THANK YOU, HOLY SPIRIT, FOR ALL YOU ARE DOING IN MY LIFE. I AM SO GRATEFUL. PLEASE FILL ME WITH YOU.

Failure

Even though the fig trees have no blossoms, and there are no grapes on the vines; even though the olive crop fails, and the fields lie empty and barren; even though the flocks die in the fields, and the cattle barns are empty, yet I will rejoice in the LORD! I will be joyful in the God of my salvation!
HABAKKUK 3:17–18 NLT

- -

Thanksgiving comes more easily when we see blessings everywhere we turn. Sometimes, though, it's hard to see the blessings. Although the spiritual world may tell a different story, the external, material world can seem pretty bleak sometimes. Sooner or later, we all have those times—times when everything we try seems to fail, times when money is tight and our bank accounts are empty, times when the physical blessings we hoped for fail to materialize. And yet even then, the prophet Habakkuk says we can rejoice! Our salvation does not rely on this world. It relies on God.

WHEN EVERYTHING SEEMS TO BE GOING
WRONG, LORD, HELP ME TO PRAISE YOU STILL.

New and Wonderful Things

O sing to the LORD a new song, for He has done wonderful things.

PSALM 98:1 NASB

- -

Just when we thought our lives would never change, when the same old problems would be following us the rest of our days, out of the blue, a breakthrough comes. God does something new and unexpected, something we never could have imagined. When that happens (and if it hasn't happened yet in your life, it will!), it's time for us to sing a new song of gratitude to God. He has blessed us in new ways—and we can find new ways to thank Him. Our God is so good to us, blessing us anew day after day, year after year.

TEACH ME TO SING A NEW SONG TO YOU,
LORD, FOR ALL THE NEW AND WONDERFUL
THINGS YOU DO IN MY LIFE.

Choices

I place before you Life and Death, Blessing and Curse.
Choose life so that you and your children will live.
And love GOD, your God, listening obediently to him,
firmly embracing him. Oh yes, he is life itself.

DEUTERONOMY 30:19–20 MSG

God gives us choices in life. We can choose ways of life and blessing—or we can choose to walk on paths that lead to destruction and pain. God doesn't punish us for our choices, but He also doesn't necessarily step in and save us from their consequences. It's up to us to pick which roads we want to follow. But why would we want to choose destruction and pain when God longs to lead us into the fullness of life? He yearns to show us a life that will fill our hearts with the deepest gratitude possible. All we have to do is follow Him.

GOD OF GRACE, THANK YOU FOR LEADING ME
TO LIFE. GIVE ME STRENGTH, COURAGE, AND
WISDOM SO THAT I MAY ALWAYS FOLLOW YOU.
I CHOOSE YOUR PATH, LORD. I CHOOSE YOU.

Wells of Salvation

With joy you will draw water from the wells of salvation.
ISAIAH 12:3 NIV

- -

Sometimes we talk as though salvation in Jesus is a thing that happens once and is done with. In one sense, this may be true, but in another sense, salvation is an ongoing thing, something that never ends. God has put "wells of salvation"—sources of life and refreshment—throughout our lives. The Hebrew word translated "salvation" in this verse meant a bunch of things: welfare, prosperity, victory, help, deliverance, health. All these things God has promised to give us, and we find them in many "wells"—in our friends and family, through prayer, through scripture, through time alone, through the beauty of nature. As we draw from them, we will be filled with joy.

THANK YOU, LORD, FOR YOUR DEEP WELLS OF SALVATION SPRINGING UP IN MY LIFE. I AM SO GRATEFUL FOR ALL THE WAYS YOU HELP ME, SAVE ME, DELIVER ME, AND MAKE ME HEALTHY.

The Earth's Song

Make a joyful noise unto the LORD, all the earth:
make a loud noise, and rejoice, and sing praise.

PSALM 98:4 KJV

The entire earth sings a song of gratitude to the Lord—and the Bible asks us humans to join in. Don't be quiet about it, says the scripture. Don't be shy. Shout out loud. Bang drums. Sing at the top of your lungs. Stomp your feet. God has done so much for us. His beauty, kindness, and love are everywhere we turn. Back in the fourteenth century, a German clergyman named Meister Eckhart said, "If the only prayer you ever said was 'thank You,' it would be enough." So make your "thank You" a joyful noise that fills your life.

LORD, I THANK YOU FOR ALL YOU HAVE DONE FOR ME. I THANK YOU FOR THE BEAUTIES OF THE EARTH, FOR THE PLEASURES OF FRIENDSHIP AND FAMILY, AND MOST OF ALL, FOR JESUS, WHO SHOWS ME YOU.

Hope and Praise

I will hope continually, and will praise You yet more and more.
PSALM 71:14 NASB

In Hebrew, the word "to praise" had to do with singing, thanksgiving, and adoration. This verse connects praise to hope. We can look at life with a gloomy outlook, expecting bad things to happen. Or we can be confident that even though bad things may happen, God is still in charge. To hope means we wait to see what God is doing. We're patient in the midst of trouble. We look forward to the day, however distant, when we will see clearly what God has been doing all along. And as we cultivate this attitude, we'll find it easier and easier to praise God.

I PRAISE YOU, GOD. I ADORE YOU. I GIVE YOU THANKS, FOR I KNOW YOU ARE WORKING OUT YOUR PERFECT WILL.

Of Him, through Him, to Him

For of him, and through him, and to him,
are all things: to whom be glory for ever.
ROMANS 11:36 KJV

Everywhere we turn, God is there. Nothing is too small or ordinary for His presence. As this verse tells us, everything is of God, everything comes to us through God, and everything is on its way to God. We often cannot see this constant process with our earthly eyes, and yet the Bible tells us it is a reality that exists all around us. Every ordinary piece of our life—computers, cell phones, commutes to work, social media, children's laughter, friends' smiles, family meals, household chores, glorious sunsets, sleepless nights, morning coffee—all of it is immersed in God. All of it is reason to give Him thanks and praise.

GOD, THANK YOU FOR ALL THE ORDINARY PIECES OF MY LIFE. THANK YOU THAT ALL THINGS ARE IN YOU.

Creation

Blessed be your glorious name, exalted above all blessing and praise! You're the one, God, you alone; you made the heavens, the heavens of heavens, and all angels; the earth and everything on it, the seas and everything in them; you keep them all alive; heaven's angels worship you!

NEHEMIAH 9:5–6 MSG

Again and again, the Bible reminds us that praise and thanksgiving are woven throughout the universe. From the earth that shelters countless wonderful creatures, to the vast seas teeming with life, to the far reaches of outer space, to the angels of heaven, all creation not only was made by God but continues to rely on Him for life. He sustains the tiny creatures found in soil and water as much as He does the angels, as much as He does us. All of us, from microbes to angelic hosts, rely on God for life.

I PRAISE YOU, LORD OF LIFE, FOR
YOUR AMAZING CREATION.

Behind the Scenes

My mouth shall tell of Your righteousness and of Your salvation all day long; for I do not know the sum of them.
PSALM 71:15 NASB

We don't know all the ways that God has come to our rescue, all the ways He has blessed us with life and well-being, for He is constantly working behind the scenes on our behalf. His care for us is ongoing, never-ending—and so our expression of gratitude also should be ongoing and never-ending. All day long, our thoughts and conversation (our inner words and outer words) should dwell on God's goodness. Gratitude should be the constant background noise of our lives.

YOU ARE SO GOOD TO ME, GOD. I'M INCAPABLE OF COUNTING ALL THE WAYS YOU HAVE BLESSED ME.

The Number Seven

Seven times a day I praise you for your righteous laws.
PSALM 119:164 NIV

The number seven in the Bible has special significance. It is the number of completeness and perfection (both physical and spiritual), and it is connected to God's creation of the world in seven days. So when the psalmist says that he praises God seven times a day, he may mean that literally, but he also means, symbolically, that praise and thanksgiving are necessary for the completion of his day. Without thanksgiving, the day would be incomplete. Gratitude expressed in praise is what gives our life meaning; it is what fulfills our days.

LORD, REMIND ME TODAY TO SAY THANK YOU TO YOU AT LEAST SEVEN TIMES!

Intergenerational Gratitude

One generation will declare Your works to the next and will proclaim Your mighty acts.

PSALM 145:4 HCSB

We pass along to our children and grandchildren many things, some of them intentional, some not. Some things we may wish we had kept to ourselves, not burdening another generation with them.

Thanksgiving could be part of our legacy to the next generation. As we make it our daily, moment-by-moment habit, the children in our lives will notice. Consciously or unconsciously, they will absorb this way of thinking and acting. The more we talk about God and express our gratitude for all His blessings, the more likely the next generations will adopt a lifestyle of thanksgiving.

LORD, I WANT TO LEAVE BEHIND A LEGACY OF GRATITUDE. TEACH ME TO BE THANKFUL CONTINUALLY.

Nothing for Granted

You lifted him high and bright as a cumulus cloud,
then dressed him in rainbow colors. You pile blessings
on him; you make him glad when you smile.

PSALM 21:6 MSG

- -

To be grateful is to recognize God's love and beauty everywhere we turn. Every breath we breathe is a gift of His love; every moment of our lives is full of His blessing. He lifts us up and makes us shine. His smile fills us with joy. When we practice gratitude, we take absolutely nothing for granted. We respond to each of life's smallest delights. Gratitude wakes us up again and again to new wonders in the world around us. As author Thomas Merton wrote, "The grateful person knows that God is good, not by hearsay but by experience. And that is what makes all the difference."

THANK YOU, LORD, FOR PILING SO MANY BLESSINGS
ON ME. MAY I TAKE NONE OF THEM FOR GRANTED.

A Spiritual Can Opener

*It is good to give thanks to the LORD and to
sing praises to Your name, O Most High.*

PSALM 92:1 NASB

"Gratitude," said the ancient Roman philosopher Cicero, "is not only the greatest of virtues, but the parent of all others." The Bible reinforces this idea, speaking again and again of thanks, praise, and gratefulness. You might say that gratitude is like a spiritual can opener that opens up our hearts to God. As our hearts open, other blessings can come into us, including the blessing of the Holy Spirit's presence within us. So make gratitude a habit. Practice it daily. May it fill your thoughts and prayers so that God in turn can bless you even more richly.

THANK YOU, LORD. I AM SO GRATEFUL TO
YOU FOR ALL YOU HAVE DONE FOR ME!

Scripture Index

OLD TESTAMENT

NEW TESTAMENT